EARLY STAGES

EARLY STAGES

Anne Jackson

LITTLE, BROWN AND COMPANY Boston ❖ Toronto

FIRST EDITION

Third Printing

Library of Congress Cataloging in Publication Data
Jackson, Anne, 1926–
    Early stages.

    1. Jackson, Anne, 1926– 2. Actors and
actresses—United States—Biography. I. Title.
PN2287.J25A34   792'.028'0924 [B] 79–328
ISBN 0-316-45501-6

RRD

Designed by Janis Capone

*Published simultaneously in Canada
by Little, Brown & Company (Canada) Limited*

PRINTED IN THE UNITED STATES OF AMERICA

DEDICATION

An Ancestral memoir for
my children, Peter, Birdie, and Kathy Wallach
and their cousins,
Judith and Gregory Egor,
Ellen, Laurie, and Russell Marz

ACKNOWLEDGMENTS

This book would never have gotten to this stage had it not been for my editor, William Phillips. He urged me on through emotional crises, and I'm grateful to him for his constancy.

To Roger Donald, editor at Little, Brown, who started me off in this venture; and the late Phyllis Jackson, the literary agent of I.C.M., whose warm and friendly support I cherish; and to her young successor, Jed Mattes, my thanks and appreciation.

I remember with warmth and gratitude the advice of my writer friend Samson Raphaelson, who read this book in an early stage and gave his sound and generous support and approval; and to my writer friends Robert Alan Aurthur; the late Audrey Gellen; Helene Hanff; Israel Horovitz; and the late Harvey Orkin, all of whom took me seriously and gave me gentle guidance.

To Beth Gray, library director, and Doris Olszewski of East Hampton Free Library, my special thanks.

To Kathleen Fisher, who typed the early manuscript, smiled, and typed some more.

To Laura Fillmore, Mr. Phillips's young assistant, for her consideration and help.

To my sisters, Kathryn Egor and Beatrice Marz, who were ready to help even though I involved them in personal memories which were painful for them.

To my children, Peter, Roberta, and Kathy, whose ancestry is made public.

To my niece, Judith Egor, who took a personal and professional interest and who gave more than I ever imagined.

And a special debt of gratitude to my friend and husband, Eli Wallach. This book cost him aggravation and lonely dinners, but he never faltered in his insistence that I continue it.

A book is not that solitary a venture after all. There are hands and hearts of others involved.

PART ONE

I tore out of my mother's body on a hot Thursday before Labor Day weekend, four years before the 1929 stock market crash. I was called Anna, thus honoring two aunts: my mother's sister Annie O'Keefe and my father's sister-in-law Anna Dobiyash. Of Mother's five babies only three survived. Beatrice (nicknamed Beady) was not quite three when I was born, but Katherine, who was seven, recalls that September third vividly.

"You were born outside of Pittsburgh in a hill town called Millvale. Dad built the house himself, and always referred to it as the House That Jack Built. Like most places we lived in, it was never finished.

"It must have been a bloody birth; I could hear the screams. The aunts were in attendance. There was Aunt Anna Dobiyash (what a saint that woman was), our Annie O'Keefe and Great-Aunt Nell Judy, who attended every birth and wake. She just sat around like a harbinger of death while the other two did all the work. They flew in and out of the house, their hands all red and wet from wringing out bedclothes.

."I peeped between the sheets drying in the yard and saw you in the clothes basket before they whisked you away down the hill in the ambulance with Mom. You had a halo of red curls on a perfectly round head. You were just beautiful, hon. The most beautiful baby ever born."

After the ambulance left, Katherine stayed behind and heard the aunts discussing Mom's labor. Great-Aunt Nell Judy was hellbent on getting a priest right away for the last rites, but Aunt Anna Dobiyash sided with Pop and made sure, in her diplomatic way, that Mom got to the hospital first. She reasoned that it was better to stop the bleeding than to worry about sanctified ground.

All Mom's births had been rough. She almost died with Katherine too, and Pop had been so concerned that he remarried her in the hospital in a religious ceremony presided over by the priest who came to hear her last confession. Their first wedding had been a civil ceremony, which had caused a furor among the relatives.

"God knows," Great-Aunt Nell Judy argued, "it was bad before, but now it's worse. I don't think Stella will make it this time. John won't do anything about getting a priest, so we'd better do it." They sent for my mother's nephew, Father Dan.

Mom pulled through but she developed a circulatory disorder; the foot became swollen and inflamed. She always referred to it as "my milk leg," because the condition happens to coincide with the time when a mother produces milk. Katherine explains, "That ulcerated foot plagued her throughout life.

"When you were brought home to the hill, poor Mom was so nervous that the least peep out of you drove her wild. Dad and I became your protectors. When you were still an infant, I remember her squeezing your cheeks when you cried and saying, 'I never wanted you, you little bitch. Stop that infernal squalling.' But when Beady hit you on the head with her baby doll — that's why you have that scar near your temple — Mom was beside herself. She really whipped Beady good. After that I had to watch you like a hawk so Beady couldn't get at you. I think you were kept on the table in the laundry basket after that."

Under Katherine's watchful eye I reached the age of four in one piece. Except for swallowing glass, drinking turpentine, and maybe stuffing beans up my nose, I was an active healthy child. The beans up the nose is one of those family incidents that gets distorted by time, being repeated so often that versions keep changing. I always thought that it was Beatrice who stuck little navy beans in her nose, but Katherine doesn't remember her doing that. "I know she had a fly in her eye that festered, and she was prone to boils. Besides, it was not a navy bean; it was a lima that got stuck."

Beady verifies the fly in the eye incident and she agrees with Katherine that it was a lima bean. "See, they're flat, hon, and it would be easier to get that kind lodged in your nasal passage." But she denies being the victim. "I definitely did not have the bean in my nose, Anne. That was you or Kay. I had enough trouble with carbuncles. I even swallowed a jawbreaker once, but beans in the nose festering and stinking . . . that wasn't me, kiddo."

My memories are clearer when we moved to Harmarville; I was about four years old. Harmarville was a summer camp for most people, but it was our year-round home. We lived in a little yellow bungalow Daddy named the "ABC" house because he'd written our initials in black paint on the eave. But Katherine contradicts this memory, too.

"Oh no, dear. You've got it wrong, all wrong," she says. "You're getting your nursery rhymes mixed. Daddy called the house in Millvale 'The House That Jack Built,' but no, there was no 'ABC' house named after us."

Beady, who is closer to my age, agrees with me: "Oh definitely. He had 'ABC' on a wooden sign. Kay's wrong about that, but don't tell her I said so. She forgets because she was christened Catherine with a C. C was her initial. She didn't get fancy with her name until Tarentum, and then it was that Kathryn business."

I thought Katherine changed the C to a K when she saw her first Katharine Hepburn movie, but I knew nothing of the Y spelling. When I ask her about this her brow arches and she says, "I've always spelled my name Kathryn. I don't know why you don't know that; and Beady is just being bratty. She's the one who was affected. Don't you remember that 'Trixy' bit she pulled?"

I am reminded that Beatrice went through the name-changing phase too. All of a sudden she renamed herself Beatrix after Princess Beatrix of the Netherlands, and nick-named herself Trixie. It didn't last too long and she dropped it after grade school.

While we lived in the "ABC" house I fell in love with Charles Lindbergh. He was every child's hero. Once a plane flew by — an event so rare in those days that it caused a sensation — and it sent me racing out the screen door leaving a grape lollipop stuck to the oilcloth beside my lunch plate. My heart bounced around, tickling my rib cage. I flew over the porch step onto the dirt walk, waving my arms frantically to the heavens and screaming, "Hi Lindy!" at the top of my lungs. That was the year Mom constantly warned Beatrice and Katherine to be sure to latch the gate so I couldn't get out.

While our parents talked of the Depression, Beady and I caught ladybugs and butterflies, jumped mud puddles on the road and went swimming in the Allegheny River. The memory of swimming came back to me with a jolt recently when Beatrice brought up the subject. "Don't you remember how Daddy would break down and cry about that swimming incident with you in Harmarville?" Beady says.

My mind begins to click. Daddy was wearing a blue swimsuit with big open loops under the arms. I wore a red wool tank suit, which itched and left red dye marks on my body.

Daddy had carried me out to where the river was deep, and when he ducked my head under, I clung to his neck so fiercely that I almost shut off his windpipe, and screamed, "I love you, Daddy, I love you. Don't drown me."

Beatrice claims that he would tell that story over and over because of the terrible guilt he must have felt.

"I think it was because of what happened to Lena," Beatrice says emphatically. "You don't remember Lena? Oh, you must, hon," she says.

"No, Beady, I don't." I cross my heart in reflex and raise my right hand up to God, as we used to do when we were children.

"Well, hon, Lena was drowned," Beady says pointedly. "She was sickly and Pop must have felt he had to do it."

Now it all falls into place; I remember Lena, a mongrel dog with reddish-brown hair and soulful eyes. Beady and I would dress her up in doll's clothes and try to wheel her in our old baby buggy. We only had the poor thing a short time. She was tied to the tree near the pump where I made mud pies. Mom once gave me a nickel because I found her wedding ring there; it had slipped off her finger when she flung out a basin of dishwater.

From these fragments of my memory I try to reconstruct my childhood. In my mind I see images and colors whirling like clothes in a dryer: the blue of a nightgown, the green of a dress, the collar to a middy blouse, a red silk tie. People and voices and names return. These are fragments I cannot lose. For other pieces of my story I must depend on the discordant memories of my sisters and other relatives. Most frustrating are the images that surface in my mind but elude me before I can hold them, much like the cloud pictures Beady and I used to paint from our imaginations. We would sit on our porch steps with jelly jars of soapy water, blowing bubbles toward the sky. "See, see," I'd scream, pointing at a cluster of soap bubbles rising into a white cloud picture, "there's a lady on a sofa with a long white boa." By the time I described the picture, the boa dissolved, the body of my lady shifted and Beady saw in it "Moses parting the heavens."

My biggest obstacle to understanding my childhood has been a psychological one. The voice of my mother's ghost comes through to me as I sit here writing; I feel her presence over my shoulder. It's as if she would reach out to grab my hand. Her voice shrills with shock and indignation. I almost revert to the child again as I defy her warnings.

"My God in heaven," she cries, "why in the name of all that's holy would you ever in this green earth dream of doing a thing like this? Time and again I warned you about sticking your nose into things that don't concern you. Now to be rummaging around in our past blabbing our business far and wide is more than a mortal can stand. Why, it's the curse of the Irish, that tongue wagging." (This was the only bad quality I had which my mother claimed for the clan.)

"What," she continues, "would possess you to do a dreadful thing like this?"

Daddy's Slavic intonations intervene. "Stella, you got to let children fly from nest. They grown now. They must swim or drown. If the Anna feels she got need to write about her experience in living, then she should do that with our blessing."

"Curiosity," Mom warns, "killed the cat."

"Curiosity," Pop insists, "is a gift. Must be deweloped. God my, Stella, we must encourage children to ask all kinds questions."

Mom didn't want me questioning her about anything, especially sex and any topic related to it, for fear my questions might rock her sense of propriety. I wasn't to pry into the fact that Aunt Nelly, whose picture I found in the old box of photographs under the bed, never had a husband but had a baby anyway.

"Where's Eileen's daddy, Mom?" I asked, having heard my cousin Joe's boy say that Eileen was a bastard. I wanted it cleared up. Even though I suspected Mom would raise Cain, some devil in me took over. I was right. She hit the ceiling. I should have known that in order to find out about sex I would have to cloak my questions behind religious definitions, like asking Mom to explain how come the Virgin Mary had an immaculate conception. The only other way to find out about sex was to ask her what the grisly headlines of the *Daily News* meant — she followed all the crime stories. I remember reading "Girl Eight Murdered," and "Little Girl's Body Found in Fiend's Lair." The words "sexually assaulted" confused and chilled my heart. When I asked Mom what that meant, she said, "It means that those men are beasts and don't you talk to any strangers whatever you do. Always ask a respectable-looking lady for directions and never accept rides from men."

"Mamma, why does God let bad men get little girls?"

"Why, God has nothing to do with it, Anna. That's the devil that gets into those animals."

"Yes, but God should be watching over us, shouldn't He, 'cause we're His sheep?"

"Well, Anna, God helps those who help themselves," Mom said with finality.

I wasn't satisfied. I wanted to know why God didn't take better care of his flock. She ended the discussion by saying, "It's God's will; now go wash your hands." We were right back where we started.

My father, on the other hand, instructed me to probe and pry and not let anything go unchallenged. He took active interest in us and constantly challenged my mother's child-rearing beliefs.

"It's their insides that have to be pretty, not what they show to outside world, Stella. You always worrying how they look and confuse the issues. They got to use their heads. Most precious thing they have. The primping makes the brain soft."

Beatrice reminds me that "Pop talked out of both sides of his mouth. He'd say real beauty is in the soul, but I can remember him teasing Mom about my nose, saying that I got that turned-up snout from her people."

Katherine winced when I mentioned this to her. "Oh, he could cut," she agreed. "When I was developing, he never let up, grabbing his head and saying to Mom, 'Oi yoy yoy. She's going to be like those roly-poly sisters of yours. I've got a heifer on my hands.'"

For my part, I remember him jumping up from the

table and pointing to me in alarm. "God my, Stella, the Anna is cockeyed."

I can hear my mother answer indignantly, "She's no such thing. If her eyes are weak, that's your side coming out. None of my people ever wore glasses." For some reason that calmed my father, but he did see to it that I went to the clinic to correct the cast in my eye.

Daddy's main concern was with our moral development. He nurtured our curiosity in oblique ways. I can still picture him walking along Liberty Avenue in Brooklyn with his grey fedora tilted at a rakish angle. He gnawed pumpkin seeds and left in his wake a trail of empty shells. We were coming home from one of our Sunday excursions, tired and weary. Beady and I walked with our arms about each other's necks. When we were tired we got giddy and affectionate. Katherine had to quicken her pace to keep up with Daddy. She all but collided into him when he stopped short, his attention riveted to some object on the ground. A quizzical look came over his face as he pointed to something on the pavement.

"Come over here, girls," he ordered. Then he pushed his hat back, shook his head and began to make little grunts. So intense was his concentration that people passing by paused momentarily to see what he was pointing to. I looked at Beady and then at Kay to see what they were looking at. Beady, twelve at the time, was impatient with Daddy's "lessons in observation." She tapped her foot and Daddy shot her a look which caused her to swiftly change her attitude. The insolence faded and she asked sweetly, "What, Daddy? What are you pointing to?"

She had disturbed his mood, and he gave himself time to recapture it, before replying, "Look there."

Katherine and I kept our eyes glued to the spot. All I saw was a huge red ant dragging a crumb of bread across a round iron disk. I suggested it was the ant. Pop was pleased and momentarily distracted. Then he said, "No, daughts." ("Daughts" was a term short for "daughter" he used to address us.)

"Is it the moss growing to one side of the iron plate?" I asked.

"Now you're warm," my father said. I could feel my heart swell with pride before Beady one-upped me.

"It's the disk, I bet. Right, Pop?" Beady piped in.

"Yep, that's what it is. Now what is meaning of?" asked Daddy, his voice cloaked with mystery. "Who put it there, do you suppose? See how is embossed with numbers? That's probably clue." He then broke the mood, turned abruptly on his heel and headed home for Sunday dinner.

We were left feeling totally frustrated at having our curiosity piqued. I wondered why he had presented the disk, as though it covered a buried treasure.

I was at his feet reading the comics that night after supper. Daddy took off his glasses, squinted at me and asked, "Well, daughts? What conclusion have you come to?"

"About what, Daddy?" I asked.

"About plate what was in pavement over there. Did you notice numbers?"

"Yes Daddy. Why?"

"Did you decipher what is **for**?"

"No."

After an interminable silence, he said, "Let me explain. Disk marks place where is underground wiring. Code numbers on plate are for power company to read so they know where is warious wires. You know who is they? Electricians from Con Edison son of mum bitch capitalists. Power should belong to all people; but never mind. One day it will. Anyway, daughts. It's wery complicated system, made easy if you know how!"

My father called himself Citizen John Jackson when he was well into wine or whiskey, but he was not a sentimental immigrant in love with his new country. He was a Yugoslav Bolshevik, testing the claims of Democracy, and he meant he was a citizen of the world.

He looms up in my memory full-blown, wearing a red tie on May Day and silencing the room with his presence when he entered. Whenever I try to describe him, I give the impression of a lovable eccentric, certainly bigger than life. Actually, he was of average height, blond with a dimple in one cheek. He had grey, almond-shaped eyes, high cheekbones, and a slight flatness at the back of his head, characteristic of his Slavic background.

He was born in 1894 in Croatia, the son of a poor shoemaker, Josip Jaksekovitch, and his wife, Katerina, who came from a well-to-do Czech family. Katerina's father felt she had married beneath her station and therefore refused her a dowry. Of Josip and Katerina's eight children, five lived, all boys.

Charles, the eldest, was left deaf after a childhood illness, so Otto, the next in line, assumed the role of big brother and protector of the others. The two youngest boys naturally paired off, which left my father, the middle child, with no real place in the family constellation. He compensated by becoming headstrong and rebellious. Daddy never got along with his mother, and as a small boy he ran away from home and stayed for days with his Czech grand-mother, who lived alone and let him help her on the farm. She had beautiful red hair and Daddy loved her.

On the rare occasions when my father talked about his past, he characterized his mother as "a dark woman, not pretty. She was stern and hard. Father was mild and gentle soul."

Nothing in the facts of my father's early life led us to believe that he ever felt "blessed or golden," as the old Croatian phrase has it. On the contrary, in his memoirs, called, curiously enough, "Joy of Finding," which he began writing near the end of his life, he says, "It's writers' profound wish to depict, without any flowering truth as it happened.

"It's son John that this novel is intended to focus on: It's him that would shorten Mother's life by many years, it was John she predicted would die on the gallows. Neither of these things happened. Mother is close to ninety and still going strong, son John is fifty-eight and never in any trouble."

His mother's prediction that he'd die on the gallows left him with a lasting sense of injury. I don't think he ever forgot the violence of those words. "Mother was tyrant," he told us.

When Otto was sixteen he was forced to leave home to avoid conscription in the Austrian army. My father, barely fourteen at the time, followed him and never looked back. "We Croats did not want to be wassals of Austro-Hungary," he explained. "We wanted indiwidual freedom, which is right of all mankind." Both boys worked their way through Europe to freedom. They went first to Germany, where Otto learned meat cutting and sausage making, earning enough money as a butcher's apprentice for them both to travel to London. There my father became interested in cosmetology and hairdressing, attracted no doubt by the degree of scientific knowledge "inwolved" in this profession. Both men had a raging, polyglot curiosity for languages. They spoke German, Hungarian, Czech, Croatian, and were excited at the prospect of adding English to the list.

My father would go on to study French, Italian, and Spanish, without ever getting beyond the primer stage. He prided himself on clear diction and a "well-modulated woice." Though self-taught, he had wide interests, not the least being elocution. He was constantly reminding us to speak in "well-modulated tones," "to pitch the woice properly ... and develop the wocabulary."

Though he never mastered the distinction between V and W himself, Daddy constantly criticized Otto's poor English. "The Otto has no wocabulary. Well, with butcher, I suppose he feels he doesn't need to express his ideas; whereas in my shop, I have customers from all walks of life. They like to conwerse."

Though Daddy loved to talk to strangers and especially other Europeans, he was reticent about discussing his past. "I'm interested in future," he would say. But I did get him to tell me about his early days in London.

"How did you get from Germany to London, Pop?" I asked.

"What do you think thumb for? Most important finger we have," he began. "You point it in direction you want to go. Necessity, Anna, is mudder of inwention; in other words, where is will is way."

"But how did you make yourself understood?"

"Oh God my, daughts. Once you know walue of hands for gesture, you speak universal language." Here, Daddy winked at me. "I had most sympathetic teacher in London. Her name was Muriel."

My mother did not like it one bit when my father teased her about Muriel. He never described her to me, but I pictured her as jolly and blonde, with apples in her cheeks; I imagined she was older than my father because when he left London in 1911, he was only seventeen. I had the impression that Muriel was "fast." After teasing Mom about her, he spoke seriously. "The Muriel was not for marrying. Not for serious consideration." In spite of my father's pretense at modern thought, indeed his early conversion to socialism and Marxism, he did not sanction "free love." Early Catholic upbringing left its mark. Though he defected and left the church at puberty, his ideas about women and how they should behave were traditional. I suspect that a passionate nature was imprisoned behind his rational facade.

Uncle Otto could not understand Daddy's erratic behavior. "Oh boy, ever since the Johnny was kid," he confided, "he was always into mischief. He gets excited, that guy, over silly things. You know when he was little fella, altar boy over there in Bjelovar, he drank priest's wine. That's his sense of humor."

Uncle enjoyed using slang expressions like "oh boy" or "toots" or "swell." It was the foreigner's need to be one of the gang.

"Sometimes he was not so funny, your Pappa," Otto said, "like time he brought home monkey for pet." Otto was referring to their early life in Pennsylvania. They lived together when they first came from London, settling in Pittsburgh with a Slavic cousin. "Oh boy, that was some roommate we had."

"Your Pappa was dapper fellow. That guy liked to spend money on clothes." A photograph of my father as a young bachelor shows him wearing a silk shirt, stiff celluloid collar and cuffs, and a cutaway jacket. The little black ribbon hanging down jauntily on his dimpled cheek is attached to his gold pince-nez. Grey spats and striped trousers, not seen in this picture, were part of his attire, according to Uncle.

"Some fancy outfit for walk monkey, eh kid?" Uncle asked as he nudged my elbow.

"Oh boy, when he brought that thing home, I said to him, 'Johnny, think twice to keep that animal. They mischief makers, and they wery dirty things.'"

"'No, no,' your Pappa argued. 'He wery well trained ... he so unusual and cute. He conwersation piece.'

"O.K. I know Johnny is stubborn. If I'm going to say, 'Don't do something ...,' to him, that's just what he's going to do. So I don't say anything.

"He learned his lesson. Monkey embarrassed him in front of crowd of people. But last straw was when that monkey did his business on your father's shoe and spoil his grey spats. Oh, I had to put my hand over my mouth when Johnny started swearing. After that he got rid of that thing.

"Fortunately for him he did. Otherwise, if your Momma ever saw Johnny come to court her with that kind of monkey business, she would have gotten so frightened, poor thing, that you wouldn't be here now."

When Daddy told the monkey story he included a detail that Otto left out. "My brudder I don't suppose told you, Anna, that he didn't like my naming pet monkey after him. I tried to explain that no insult was intended; that we all descended from the ape. He got wery poor sense of humor, or else he should read the Darwin. Well, as Einstein says, it's all relative."

The most serious rift between the brothers occurred over Pop's tearing all over the countryside on a motorcycle. After a second accident with the machine, Otto flatly refused to lend his brother any more money.

"You know, Annie," Otto said, "I had to talk rough to that guy to make him realize it was for his own good. Your Momma cried to me for help, poor thing. She was in sidecar with your sister Katrin and the Johnny was racing around those hills like crazy. She threw baby to safety when the Johnny nearly crashed into tree. I said, 'Johnny, get rid of that buggy what you riding or I don't lend you one cent.' He wouldn't talk to me for months, but finally saw the light."

Obviously, the light he saw failed to put him on his course. "He had gypsy blood," Otto said, "and he was always going from job to job and moving from place to place." After I was born, he made an attempt to settle down by accepting a position in a fancy emporium, Joseph Horn and Co. in Pittsburgh, where he was to work as a hairdresser. My mother was so proud when my father landed that job. It paid well, there were fringe benefits, and her youngest sister, Gert Murray, worked as a stenographer for the company.

But he was there for less than a year when he had one of his blowups with authority.

"John had already been warned about being difficult," Aunt Gert said. "I kept hearing those awful things about him. He was never one to listen, you know. You just couldn't tell him anything. I saw him in the elevator one day and I said, 'John, you're not to tell a living soul that we're related. Don't ever let on that you know me. Why, it might cost me my job.' "

My father, though very hurt, was not put on his guard by her warning. One day a lady customer sashayed into the salon in her short skirt and cloche hat and asked for a "bob" (Clara Bow and Billie Dove were all the rage then). She warned him coyly, "Not too short, now . . . leave me some to curl." But Pop used his own judgment about the haircut. He kept shearing her neck, clicking his scissors and piling shreds of hair on the white smock. He grabbed time by the forelock and cut that lady's hair clean off her head. When he spun her around for a look at the back view, she threw the hand mirror across the room and in a frenzy, spurting invectives, she left the room, causing all heads to turn.

Daddy was given his walking papers. The phenomenal salary (with tips) of seventy-five dollars per week came to an abrupt halt and he was never able to reach such financial heights again. Our mother's dream of his settling into an establishment went up in smoke. Our house was sold, thus starting a succession of moves.

The next move put my father into the manufacturing business and into jail. He had gone into partnership with a landsman, making and bottling Bandoline, a preparation which glued the hair to your head in finger waves if you were a woman, and into a slicked-down Rudolph Valentino gloss-head if you were a man. John was in the process of making his fortune on this and related products when the rift with his partner, Sodorovitch, came. The dissolution of the partnership was not friendly. My father sued, lost the case, and for not observing the judge's calling for "order in the court," was given a few days in confinement to think about his conduct. Mom had to visit him in jail, Katherine tells me. "Can you imagine how mortified she must have been?"

"I wonder why she went, then," I say.

"To bring him his clean white shirt," my sister answers, annoyed at my obtuseness.

On Daddy's release, the moving vans came to cart us to a new house and our father to a new business arrangement. He packed up all his hairdressing equipment, taking scores of bottles and pellets of quince seeds with him. He had new labels printed up with pictures of kewpie-doll-mouthed flappers and suave, thin-lipped men. The "Marvel Hair Products" poster was placed in the window of his new shop in Tarentum. It was 1931 and Dad ran one of the first unisex hairdressing parlors.

I remember my first haircut there. Daddy lifted me onto the barber chair, spun it around and then cranked it up. I didn't like the manipulating of my head up and down or the sensation of barber shears on my neck, but I liked the perfumy smells of the lotions and the colored bottles which lined the shelves. Pink and green and red substances reflected their colors on the white walls, danced in the sunlight, doubled their images in the big Pittsburgh plate-glass mirrored walls. A few potted ferns and hardy snake plants grew in the window near the barber pole. Daddy kept his shop immaculately clean, never allowing hair to pile up for long on the black and white checkerboard floor. On a little ivory-colored child's table, Daddy displayed his magazines and placed his telephone. It was there in Tarentum that he had another serious altercation with the law, this time for refusing to display the American flag on a national holiday.

A Patrolman Kern sauntered into Pop's shop and said, "Hey, Jackson, I don't see your flag out. What gives?"

Pop countered, "You don't see, because there's nothing to see. So, that's accurate obserwation, officer."

"What the hell are you talking about anyhow, Jackson? Don't get smart with me. Now you act as though you understand our language ..."

"Yup," Pop interrupted. "I understand language all right." His hackles went up.

"You do, huh," said Kern. "Well, let me tell you something. In this country you obey the law. You follow the examples set by the other merchants in the town, and you show respect for our flag."

"Yeah, well," Pop winced and said with exaggerated patience, "I like to know reason for things and to accommodate out of right spirit. Now, I suppose you know historical facts and all of that? What is reason for flag waving?"

"The law is the reason, Jackson. I'm not going to stand here and argue with you. You obey the law."

Patrolman Kern tried not to show his rage. He swallowed hard, looked out the window, then toward the mirror, saw his face redden, tapped his stick in the palm of his hand and said with controlled anger, "By this afternoon, Jackson, I want to see your flag out; then we'll take it from there, fair enough?" He turned and left, placing a tongue in his cheek and shook his head in disbelief as he passed the shop window.

In the lull following Kern's departure, Daddy sat in the barber chair and read the papers, which were full of the food riots and cartoons of "Hoover Flags," empty pockets turned inside out. (The "Hoover Hogs" were jackrabbits shot by farmers for food.)

Daddy went to the five-and-dime on his lunch hour and purchased a tiny paper flag. He shoved it into the earth of the rubber plant in his window. Then he scrubbed the earth out from under his nails and greeted his third customer of the day, Mr. Dolitch, a fine-spoken gentleman with whom Pop discussed Darwin's theories and the class struggle, capitalism and music. "Mr. Dolitch is a wery intelligent and sensitive person," Pop said. "He studied wiolin over there in Hungary, but for make living he had, of course, to become worker. He's got job in mill. How long it lasts, we don't know."

As Daddy wiped the soap from Karl Dolitch's neck, Patrolman Kern came into the doorway, signaled for attention, and then began raising and lowering his bulk on the balls of his feet. He hit his palm rhythmically with his club and said, "O.K., Jackson, where is it?"

My father's mouth curled up slightly as a sense of victory came over him. He danced around his customer in his white starched uniform, "plié"ing and clicking his scissors as though he wore castanets. "Over there in window," he scissor-pointed.

The patrolman looked. The blood rose and flooded his face. "Where, Jackson?" he inquired suspiciously.

My father, not giving an inch, slid the comb under Mr. Dolitch's hair near his ear, and explained, "Look there, where is plant on side where pole is. Go on, walk over there to window — you going to see flag."

Officer Kern looked and exploded. "What the hell's the big idea, Jackson?"

"Well," Daddy said as he continued his ballet around Dolitch, "I am going to explain to you what idea is. I don't know about *big* idea because I'm dealing in not so big things. You want big flag. My business is not so big. You want big show of patriotism. I can't afford big show of patriotism. My children are not so big. They can't work to help pay rent. I can afford little things. So that's reason I have little flag."

When Mom got wind of this, she threw some things in a suitcase, took me by the hand, and we went home to Grandma's.

My mother was christened Stella Germain Murray in 1895 by an Irish Catholic priest in a Roman Catholic church in Pittsburgh, Pa. Her mother, Mary Ann, one of the Summerses of Buena Vista, had strains of Scotch and English in her blood line, but Michael Murray, my grandfather, was Irish through and through. He came from Roscommon, Ireland, and worked as pit foreman in the coal mines outside Pittsburgh. The Murrays never referred to themselves as "working class" people. "Poor but proud" was the expression they used no matter how shanty Irish they seemed.

Grandmother was called "Ma'am" ever since I can remember, a respectful form of address that became the name she was always known by. It is difficult to imagine that that small, pretty woman with dainty hands and feet who was noted for her fine white teeth and good manners could give birth to eleven Murray children, nine of whom survived. My mother was seventh of the brood of six girls and three boys. Though her place in the family, like my father's in his, was undistinguished, she never severed relations with her family, as my father had. She was very attached to her "people," as she called them, and especially to Ma'am.

Ma'am was looked up to and respected by her children, in-laws, grandchildren, and fellow townspeople alike. Grandma had a way of commanding respect without ever having to ask for it. Her eyes had a beguiling twinkle. On rare occasions I would spot that same twinkle in my mother's eye and then I knew I could coax her into doing something I wanted. But Grandma's twinkle was different. She could have been a great diplomat or gambler because she never betrayed by as much as a bat of the eye what she was thinking. Any gossip and backbiting that went on around her was soon quelled by the force of her silence.

She always wore a little straw hat, gloves, and powder when she went out. Her skin, like my mother's, couldn't take a hint of sun. A proper lady, Mrs. Murray, and everybody thought so.

Stella tried in every way to imitate her mother. She groomed herself exactly like Ma'am except for the black mourning dress that Ma'am always wore. But the likeness stopped there. "Stella is her father through and through," all the relatives said and Great-Aunt Nell Judy decreed, "There's not a drop of Summers blood in Stella's veins. She's a Murray down to the marrow, high-strung and touchy just like the rest of them."

My Grandfather, or "Pap," as he was called, was a person who could make even the bravest quake. Though he died before I was born, his presence was still very much felt in Ma'am's house. In fact, all the departed souls of Mom's family, and there were quite a few of them, were talked of and gossiped about along with the living. Ma'am's parlor had seen many a casket, but Grandpa's spirit reigned supreme there. His portrait dominated the tiny room that was his darkened shrine. The cornflower blue eyes stared out from a large oval gilt frame, and the relatives swore on the Bible that whoever tinted that picture captured Pap's coloring to a T. He had a thick bush of auburn hair and a bright red handlebar moustache. My mother's hair changed to a chestnut brown as she got older, but her cornflower blue eyes and violent temper were without a doubt inherited from her father. All his other children and practically all his grandchildren inherited his red hair.

Whenever we entered that parlor, Mom's lip began to tremble and she lowered her voice as she directed my attention to Pap's portrait. I was both impressed and intimidated by the image of the man looking out from behind the convex glass. I remember thinking once that his moustache twitched, but it was just the play of light and shadows caused by vibrations from a passing streetcar. Everything in the room seemed to move, including Grandpa's big chair, which no one ever sat in from the day he died. I thought it was from fear of catching some disease, but Mom corrected that false impression.

"My God in heaven, child," she said, "What would possess you to think a thing like that? Pap was never sick until the day he was taken."

I was afraid to ask her in his presence how he went.

I always suspected that Mom was afraid of her father, but her reluctance to talk about her past came from diffidence and not, as in my father's case, from pent-up resentments.

If anything, she was tied to her family's apron strings, so much so that when it came time for her to leave home at the age of sixteen, she went straight from scrubbing Ma'am's floors to scrubbing her sister Maggie's. Maggie, like Ma'am, birthed a baby every year, so the housework must have been very heavy. It was not uncommon in 1911 in large Irish families for married sisters with means to take in less fortunate members.

Even though my father called such an arrangement exploitation, he liked Aunt Maggie, who everybody, including my mother, said had Ma'am's wonderful disposition and kind ways. So my mother was grateful to be under the wing of her own flesh and blood no matter how tough the going was.

"Why, my God in heaven," one of her other sisters said, "Thank God our Stella worked for Maggie. Look what happened to our poor sister Nelly. She was a mere fifteen when she was thrown into the hands of a lascivious old widower ... working her fingers to the bone for that old reprobate and all she got in return was a child born out of wedlock and he never even showed up for her wake." The child of that unholy union, orphaned at birth, was in turn made to work as an indentured servant for the family that took her in.

During the four years my mother toiled away for her sister, rumor had it that she became engaged to a farmer, Jim Mahoney, but broke off with him when Pop came along in his cutaway jacket, silk shirt, and buffed fingernails, smelling of hair tonic. My mother, Pop said, was quite a beauty when they met. I pictured her with long wavy hair, which she pinned into a soft bun at the nape of the neck. She had the classic peaches and cream complexion; her cheeks had a slight natural tearose look and they were as velvety as the fuzz on a peach. She was tall — about 5′5″ — and slim compared to the rest of her sisters, and her legs were well shaped. She had all her own teeth then. The gold bridgework was put in early in her marriage, a lifetime reminder of Dad's prosperous days.

I'm sure Mom thought that Pop was a city slicker and gave up her farmer for him to avoid being stuck in the backwoods somewhere milking cows and lugging chicken feed. She saw the role of farmer's wife as the life of a dolt, and she referred to country houses as "Godforsaken hovels."

The circumstances surrounding my parent's first meeting was meant to be a closely guarded secret. No amount of coaxing or nagging from my sisters or me could get her to tell how she and Daddy had met. One fateful night, however, with all the windows open so the neighbors could hear, Daddy in an exuberant mood loudly announced that the advertisement he'd put in the paper "was worth every penny spent. Never in my wildest dreams did I dare hope when I wrote 'cultured young man, intentions honorable, looking to make acquaintance of young lady' that this beautiful Irish colleen would answer my cry from the soul."

Mom, enraged by this betrayal, turned on him in a fury and flung her ladle at him. "I wish to God I had never set eyes on you, John. I'm leaving with Anna in the morning. I'll never forgive you for this."

My sisters and I sat in stunned silence at the table. Daddy retrieved the ladle. He winked at us, giggled, and whispered, "Oh, God my, now I put foot into it. I shouldn't of let cat out of bag. The wifey doesn't like it. She's bashful, poor thing."

We left my father so often that the visits merge. Although I didn't like it when my parents fought, I loved running home to Ma'am's with our suitcase, for Mom's relatives were a colorful lot. They were constantly birthing, burying, and backbiting. They wet-kissed, were maudlin and sentimental. Mom was very much at home with them.

One particular visit stands out. I was not more than four or five. We arrived at Grandma's and Mom was red-eyed and crying. Grandma had just gotten the men off to work, "the men" being Uncle Vincent, Mom's older bachelor brother, and Ma'am's other son, Uncle Jimmy, who was "not right" but who worked in the steel mills anyway, even though he could be seen in the alley talking to himself. They always said that Jim was "gassed in the war," as though that was the reason for his odd ways. I guess the truth was that Uncle Jim was brain-damaged. I never had a talk with him but I always had the feeling he was Grandma's favorite son, so I liked him too. We always smiled at one another, although I now suspect he wasn't smiling at me in particular, but rather always had that expression on his face.

Aunt Mary Deemer, Mom's sister who lived across the courtyard from Grandma's and was a woebegone woman, saw everything that was going on from her back porch. Just as soon as Mama and I set foot in Grandma's kitchen, Aunt Mary came wending her way through the neighbor's clothesline to get to Ma'am's kitchen door.

"Is our Stella here, Ma'am?" she called en route.

"Yes, uh-huh, she is. She just arrived, Mary. Come in. Close the door good. There's a draught this morning." Ma'am was very patient and even-tempered with everyone.

"Which girl's this, Ma'am?" Aunt Mary asked, jigging toward me. She always pretended with children that she didn't know who you were. She wanted you to think you'd grown so much she didn't recognize you.

"Now stop being silly, Mary," Grandma said evenly. "Why, that's Stella's youngest girl. That's little Anna." Ma'am wore her grey man's sweater like a shawl over her frail little shoulders. "Aren't you chilled, Mary, running over here without your warm clothes on?"

Aunt Mary's attention was fixed on me. "Is that little Anna?" she lisped. Her false teeth, never properly fitted, jiggled in her mouth. "Come here to me, honey, and let's see how big you've got. Don't be bashful now. Come over and give uth a kith." Her invitation caused me such embarrassment that all my coordination went awry. I dreaded the spittle on my hot cheek, and the deafeningly loud smack of her kisses.

When I finally forced myself over to my aunt and suffered being in her clutches, she asked sneakily, the little grey eyes dancing mischievously, "Did your daddy and your mother have another falling out?"

"Here, Mary, don't be asking the child a thing like that," Ma'am said instantly, a mite annoyed. "John will be here tomorrow to get them. He always lets just a little time go by." The last two times Mom and I had left him, he came and got us. I don't even think anything was said. He just came to the house, hat in hand, and took our suitcase. I grabbed for his free hand and he squeezed mine in recognition. "Why don't you go to your George now, Mary? Stella's a little upset, but maybe she'll be feeling better by supper," Grandma said.

Aunt Mary really hated having to go, but Ma'am had a way of controlling her children, a knack neither Aunt Mary nor my mother inherited.

"Well, if you need me to take little Anna for a while, I will," Aunt Mary volunteered.

"Do you want to go with your Aunt Mary?" Ma'am asked. "She might have crullers over there with jelly in them."

I lowered my eyes and shook my head. I really only liked to go to Aunt Mary's if her oldest girl, Minnie, was there with her fella. But Minnie was at work and her sisters were at school, and anyway, I wanted to hang around and hear Mom tell Ma'am about her trouble with Daddy.

When Aunt Mary left, my mother came to the top of the stairs and asked, "Was that the door slamming, Ma'am?"

"Yes, come on down now, Stella, and I'll fix you some tea."

"Would you have some bread and butter, Anna?" my grandmother asked. "I've not much in the house, except the men's supper." Grandma was not stingy, but she kept a close watch on her larder. Since the men and Aunt Gert lived at home and paid board, they got the best.

I loved being invited to tea and when Mom came down, we sat at table together. It was exciting to be in on everything.

Ma'am went about her own business, brewing the tea, cutting and thinly buttering the bread. She sprinkled some sugar on top of mine and then coaxed my mother to "eat a little something." Then she settled herself at the round table. "Here, come on now, Stella, have some bread and butter with your tea. There's some fine peach preserves in that jar." She poured some tea into her saucer and began to sip it.

I watched Mom bite into her bread and her eyes brimmed up before she could swallow. She spat the lump of bread in her hand. Ma'am turned her eyes away and winced ever so slightly.

"Oh Ma'am," she said, "ever since the children were little, he's done nothing but move us about. And now he's bought this house in this awful place. He never let on that he was doing such a thing till it was done. Why, I'm just too ashamed. Job's Hole is where all the colored people are, in the backwoods. He just wants all that land for gardening."

This was the first time I heard about this particular move to another town in the back hills, only a mile or so from where we lived at the time.

"Well, Stella, it may not be as bad as you think. You know John's a good man. I guess in the old country those people didn't have much either. They all seem to want their own land."

"I should have married Jim Mahoney. Instead of growing those old flowers, which don't do a bit of good, at least Jim would have raised vegetables for us to eat."

I got confused at my mother's mention of another man. My grandmother placed her freckled hand on mine. "Don't be saying that, Stella. Why, Anna will think you mean it."

"Well, I do mean it, Ma'am. That child knows too much for her age already. Why, do you know what that man did in front of her just last night? That's another reason I'm here, and I'm not going back."

"Now Stella, you've got a good man there. He's always been a good provider. He's your husband and you'll just have to put up with his ways."

"I'll not put up with his drinking, Ma'am, as God's my witness. He never used to drink but now it seems every Saturday night . . . I knew the minute he walked in that door last night with his hat askew. I had been on my sore foot cooking and scrubbing my fingers to the bone all day long and I had such a good meal prepared for him. And he just let our supper get cold because he was full of moonshine. I told him so too, didn't I, Anna? I said, 'If that's moonshine on your breath, John, why you can go back to where you got it.' Then he just started acting real foolish, trying to hug me at the hot stove and then hopping on one foot showing the girls how sober he was; and then telling them about how we met and with the blinds up and the neighbors seeing in. I rue the day I set eyes on him," Mom wailed. "I rue it."

The recollection made my mother blush and gush a fresh batch of tears.

Ma'am poured us all some more tea, sighed and said, "Well, it's hard to think what troubles a man."

"Yes, but he was so foolish telling the children all about us. Why, I was mortified."

"Oh, now, Stella, people meet by all kinds of arrangements. That's not anything to be touchy about."

"When he gets that drink in him, Ma'am, you can't believe the way he acts. Anna here is witness to what went on."

Mom didn't realize that as a witness that night, I was thrilled to hear Pop rhapsodize about meeting her.

From my youngest day I felt the tensions between my parents, so it came as no surprise when years later Aunt Gert, my mother's youngest sister, said that they were ill-matched.

"Oh, they loved each other but they were ill-matched. Your father had so many interests; he had a fine mind, but he was restless. Stella just didn't understand him. She wanted a nice home and nice things for you girls. The wisest thing John did was to move you to New York. You've all met the right men and had good lives. But of course, for Stella, that move was a calamity."

John and Stella remained as different as day is from night. It wasn't just a clash of personalities; the tension was noticeable on every level. In everyday life it manifested itself in small differences. For example, Daddy ate black bread, Mama white; he loved sauerkraut, she said vinegar thinned the blood; he drank tea in a glass with lemon and Mama had hers in a cup with milk. (That should have gone unnoticed, but it bothered my mother because it wasn't Irish.) There was constant friction between them about money, booze, and life-styles.

When we moved far away and could no longer run home to Ma'am, Mom would threaten to leave him and get a job. But there was no escape for her as far as I could see — she had three children, a leg that crippled her, and only a grade school diploma. So she bit her nails, held back the tears, and read crime stories in the newspapers.

Until Cousin Minnie died, the only person I knew in heaven was Grandpa. I had never seen him in the flesh, so his soul leaving his body and floating up to heaven where he'd live forever as an angel in Paradise was quite an acceptable fate to me. It wasn't until the death of my cousin, whom I'd known all my life, that the description of the body as just an envelope for the soul — to be disposed of in the ground and thought of as so much dust — imposed an intolerable strain on my young mind.

We were still in Harmarville at the "ABC" house when the news came. I was making mud pies in the yard near the pump. Thelma Werner ran over from the town store.

"Tell your mother it's a call from McKeesport, Anna Jane."

My mother appeared at the screen door as though summoned, her face already alert and anxious.

"It's a call from McKeesport, Stella," Thelma said, holding the gate open for my mother.

"Oh my God," I heard my mother's voice trail. "I hope to God it's not anything to do with Ma'am."

I lined my mud pies on the porch steps to dry in the sun. The noon whistle blew and I jumped on a rung of the gate to swing on while waiting for Mother.

When she returned, her eyes were all red and teary. She pinched at the drops which formed at the tip of her nose.

"Your sisters will be home for lunch soon, so go wash

your hands at the pump," she said, "and come in and have your soup. Don't let the flies in." Her voice broke. "That . . . that was Uncle George. Your Cousin Minnie died."

At lunch I watched the white buttered bread floating in my tomato soup and listened to the remarks my mother addressed to my sister Katherine: "Your Uncle George called. All he said was, 'Stella, your sister Mary's bad. We lost our Minnie last night. It was her heart.' " In the silence which followed, Beady and I slurped our soup. "And her engaged to be married and all. If there was a God in heaven," she railed, "He would have spared our Mary this. Why, my God almighty, she's lost those two boys already. You'd think that would be enough."

"What boys, Mamma, what happened?" I wanted to know.

"Our cousins, stupid. We have dead cousins," Beady hastened to inform me.

"Oh it's awful," Mom said, "both her boys were taken before their time. First it was Mike, who lied about his age to get in the army and then he went and got himself killed over there in the Great War. Such a good-looking boy too —blond like Uncle George. And then there was little James; he was run over by a train when he was no bigger than our Anna here. He had red curly hair and was real smart for his age. Our poor Mary doesn't even have a picture left of him."

"Well, what happened, Mama?" I insisted. I already felt uneasy about him being my age, and his having red hair added to my discomfort.

"Well," Mom continued, "he had a sore toe with a bandage on it, and he was crossing the railroad tracks in Scotchville to get to the company store. There was this woman putting on her corset and she saw little Jim from her window. She could have saved him, but it wouldn't have been decent to run out like that. You'd think she could've thrown something on. The train bounced his little body up and down three times and three pennies were found in his little clenched fist. I guess he was going for candy . . . and now poor Minnie, my God, it's just not right," Mom said before she lost control. I began to sob sympathetically for her.

Although our mother appeared deeply religious, she rebelled at certain doctrines of her faith. She never truly accepted "God's will" unconditionally. But when she was challenged by my father that evening for wanting to take me to the funeral with my two older sisters, she became indignant. "Why, she has to pay her last respects, John," she argued. "Minnie's a blood relation and God's will is God's will." And so it was. I was delighted to be going with my mother and sisters to my first funeral.

The next morning was hectic. Mamma got up early and ironed dresses and underwear for the days ahead. The big black suitcase sat on the chair next to the ironing board with its mouth open. I wanted to put in my paper dolls and jacks but Mamma said, "Take those right out, Lady Jane. A wake is no place to play at."

"You bet your sweet life," Daddy mumbled; "there's no playing there, Anna. That's serious business, that black magic that you going to see."

"Now don't start up, John," Mamma said.

Beady came in, carrying her green organdy dress. "You'll not wear that, Beady. You can't wear organdy to a wake. Hang it right back up." Katherine sneaked around the ironing board and nagged my mother about a black dress. "Wear something navy, Katherine," Mom said. "Why nobody expects a girl your age to own a black dress anyway."

"What hocus-pocus is this, Katherine," Pop asked. "You twelve years old in black? I think leave girls at home, Stella. They gonna be sleeping all over place there, carrying back bedbugs."

Mom shouted angrily, "Don't you dare talk like that about my people. I won't stand for it with Little Minnie gone."

Pop then mumbled about "Irish looking forward to funerals same as children look forward to Christmas."

Mom grew livid. "I'd sooner walk to the station than ride with you," she cried. "Get your hats and coats, girls." Tears of anger and self-pity rolled down her cheeks as she left the house. We all trudged along after her, looking back to see if Poppa would follow. Mamma kept switching her heavy suitcase from hand to hand. When we turned the bend onto the cinder road, the motor from our Ford sounded. "Don't any of you get into that car with him," she threatened. "Mind!"

Poppa passed us and stopped a few yards ahead. He walked over to Mamma and reached for the suitcase. To my amazement, she surrendered it without a word and we all got in the car. We boarded the train at the station. Beady and I sat on the plush green window seats facing each other so that the soles of our shoes touched. I looked out the window and saw my father tip his hat to my mother. A look of compassion came into his eyes, which caused my mother to grab for her hanky. The train gave a lurch and we were off to McKeesport.

We arrived for the wake train-weary and were taken into the darkened parlor. I could not believe that the statue in the coffin was really Minnie, who Mamma used to say was "just like her mother ... sloppy."

"She's always clopping around in bedroom slippers and with her hair uncombed. And don't sleep at Aunt Mary's when you go to Grandma's. I don't want you carrying home bedbugs."

But I used to sleep there anyway every chance I got, for I loved being with Minnie. I would have to restrain myself from waking her until noon though I longed to have her get up and take me to the stores and to Icaly's, the Howard Johnson's of Pittsburgh.

The last time I visited, I sat on the edge of her bed and coughed and sighed for her attention until she woke up. "What time is it?" she said, wincing as she tasted her morning breath. She smiled wanly and reached for a cigarette. I watched her draw in the first cloud of smoke. It disappeared in her mouth and then a thin stream crawled out of her pointy nose. She blew smoke rings on my fingers and laughed shrilly when they flattened out like airless inner tubes. I had never seen a woman smoke in real life before and I was intrigued by her boldness.

She lifted herself from the bed, scratched her stomach and headed for the bathroom. I followed and perched myself on the toilet seat so I could watch her apply face paint. She handed me her cigarette to hold and I placed it carefully between my fingers and watched it burn. A little red ring swirled around, forming a gray ash. I blew at it to make it smoke. When she did her cupid's bow, I stood on the toilet seat so I could see better. In two sure sweeps, the bow was made and she pressed the red of the upper lip onto the lower. She penciled her brows like Marlene Dietrich, high over her eyes like two hills. Then she raised her cheeks in a fake smile and applied rouge with a red-stained powder puff.

"Remind me to get a new one when we pass the five-

and-dime," she said as she tossed the puff aside. She asked my opinion about what she should wear and carefully explained why she couldn't wear the fancy dress I'd chosen. "That's too good to slop around in, honey," she said as she selected a brown crepe dress that had faded to orange at the armpits and pulled it over her wrinkled slip.

"Aren't you going to change your petticoat?" I asked from under the bed where I scrambled for her shoes.

"Nobody sees your underwear, honey," she answered as she squeezed her bare feet into the black pumps. She showed me a combful of blonde hair, saying, "If this keeps up, I'll be bald."

Minnie changed her mind about the powder puff. She bought ruby lipstick instead and then we went to Icaly's for ice cream. We vowed we'd taste every flavor on the long list.

I wanted to get a better look at Minnie in her casket, but the room was dark and there were all those people in black standing around whispering with ooh's and ah's, voices shaken with grief, hushed and breaking into sobs — people losing control and running out, followed by others who tried to comfort them.

Minnie looked small in her casket of white satin. Her wedding dress and satin slippers just seemed to blend into the folds of the box. She looked as limp as a pillow doll. The blonde marcelled hair was haloed by lots of white veiling. Her mouth was painted ruby red and it made her nose look sharper for some reason. The nostrils were pink as a rabbit's. The gold and pearl rosary which was threaded through her fingers belonged to Joe Kelly's mother. All the relatives commented on how beautiful it was.

Joe Kelly, her intended, stayed kneeling at her coffin, his hands clasped in prayer. The smells of flowers, burning candles, and mothballs all seemed to exude from his heaving figure. I realized later that it was Uncle George and not Joe smelling up the room with camphor, because Uncle only got out of his undershirt and suspenders and into a suit on special occasions.

Not only was it unusual to see Uncle George dressed up and walking about, but the wake brought all kinds of food into Aunt Mary's kitchen as well. I recall Grandmother serving everybody and quietly scooping crumbs from the table into her hand. All the aunts came, so there was a dizzying repetition of names. At least two or three if not four relatives answered to the same name and there were "big" and "little" everyones. When that description was exhausted, we were referred to as Peggy's Annie, not Stella's, or Jenny's John, not Joe's. Grandma seemed to be the only one who kept them all straight. There was much drinking, tea poured into saucers, condensed milk and sugar, and slurping and gagging as emotion swelled.

Groups of relatives and neighbors came and went and Aunt Mary recounted for each group the tale of Minnie's death.

Consolations flew around the table from my other aunts.

"She was a good girl."

"A better girl never lived."

"As true as there's a God in heaven, little Minnie's there."

Aunt Mary continued, "Well, a' Friday she came home from work and went straight upstairs to lie down. I went up and asked what the matter was. She hadn't touched a morsel of food and I thought maybe she had an upset stomach. And mind you, she never let on what the matter was. She was like that, Minnie was. Never gave in to an illness. Well, a' Saturday, she got up pale as a ghost and came down to breakfast. I mind she sat in the chair you're sitting in now, Stella."

The association brought a lump to my mother's throat. Once more the little chants went around the table.

"She always loved Stella."

"Looked a lot like Stella as a girl."

"No, she was the spitting image of George," Aunt Annie contradicted, and there was an edge to her voice.

"Oh yes, she looked like her father."

"Never letting on she was sick," Aunt Mary continued. "Oh, she was good."

"I mind how she loved sweet potatoes, always asked if there were any when she was down in Braddock."

"The Lord takes His own, Mary," my Aunt Josie said.

"I guess He knows best," Aunt Mary agreed. "Still . . . Well, anyway, a' Sunday morning I went in to see how she was feeling. I hadn't slept a wink that night. I sat on the edge of the bed and held her hand. 'Mom,' she said, 'I'm not going to live. I saw a white dove on the window sill.' "

"Oh my, that's a good omen. They say if you have to go, that Sunday is the best day," Aunt Annie said. "As sure as God's in heaven, she's a saint."

" 'I saw a white dove on the sill, Mom.' Those were her very words," Aunt Mary repeated, pursing her mouth and blinking for emphasis.

Uncle George finished the story. "Five minutes later she was gone."

In the silence that followed, Aunt Nell Judy said, "When I sat up with her last night, two little rosebuds appeared on the candles. It was after midnight, and Joe had just gone home. Oh, that poor boy! He'll never marry, you know. He swears he'll never find anyone to replace his Minnie."

All the aunts chimed in at once to concur with Great-Aunt Nell Judy. "Oh, he was wild for Minnie. I just feel for that poor man."

"I can't believe that Minnie's gone," someone keened. "Why she seemed so full of life, and all that money for a wedding gown." This remark just lay heavy in the air until someone tried to save the moment. "Never mind, she would have made a beautiful bride."

"She'll be buried with her ring on," Aunt Mary said. "Joe insists on it."

Daddy was right — makeshift beds laid in Ma'am's room. Just a pillow and a blanket thrown on the floor. The rug smelled musty and the floor was hard, and I was terrified they'd turn the hall light out. That night I dreamed that Minnie turned into Mamma, that she was alive and we were eating ice cream cones when she let go of my hand, and I couldn't find my way back home through Strawberry Alley. It got later and later and something was following me, but I couldn't scream or make a sound. I woke in the night scared to death and sorry I had come. I hated the funeral and people mourning, but most of all I hated death. I climbed up to Grandma's bed, where my mother was sleeping. "Mind you don't kick my sore foot," she whispered, "and don't wake Ma'am." In the moonlight I could see my Grandmother's wavy white hair unbraided. She breathed through her mouth and I felt my mother's cheek all damp from tears against mine.

Minnie was buried on the fifth day. Aunt Mary, near collapse, tried to jump into the grave. Joe Kelly had to be restrained. Uncle George for the first time broke down and cried like a baby. All this was recounted around the table once again before we went home. Great-Aunt Nell Judy's elaboration of the little red roses that appeared around the candles of Minnie's casket so inflamed my sister Katherine's imagination that it gave her the courage to admit that when she walked through the parlor the night before, she too had seen the roses and Cousin Minnie had winked at her.

Great-Aunt Nell Judy was the most mystical of all the aunts. It was generally accepted among my mother's people that Great-Aunt could see "something" no one else saw or was likely to see. While the authenticity of the supernatural world was unquestioned by my aunts and cousins, the power of sight into it was considered a rare and wonderful thing. Thus, Katherine's visions of Minnie were dismissed as hallucinations and my own fanciful and mystical experiences were treated with equal skepticism. It is probably just as well, because so vivid was my imagination as a child that I could easily have embraced and become lost in a world of ghosts and Irish superstition if given encouragement. The exclusivity of the visionary turf on my mother's side along with my father's skepticism eventually steered me onto a more rational path.

Nevertheless, it was always thrilling and a little frightening to visit Great-Aunt Nell Judy and there is no doubt that her "powers" were a profound stimulus to my own visions. She spent summers on a tugboat on the Allegheny River, where she told fortunes and sold pots and pans. In the fall and winter she kept house up in the hills of a section referred to as Irish Town — the only names you ever heard there were Duffy or O'Flaherty. She was an O'Keefe of the Black Irish. Her hair, with a strand of white running dramatically through it, was parted in the middle with razor-sharp accuracy; her little eyes were stuck in like coals in a snowman's head. She had small rounded teeth with milky white spots in a little red mouth, and skin as smooth as a baby's. Her delicate features, including her tiny perfect nose, were all out of proportion to the rotund face and figure.

Suffering from a milk leg like my mother, she too wore the familiar elasticized rubber stocking. Together they commiserated and massaged their legs, swaying rhythmically. "A woman's lot, Stella . . . since I lost my man . . ." (She was referring to Great-Uncle Pat.) "His going is the worst thing I had to bear. And then to be punished like that with its birth." The "it" was a son, talked about in hushed tones so as not to reach "big ears in little heads." The most we heard was that her son was not right and had to be put away. No one ever mentioned where.

It was the joy of my life and Beady's to visit her. Although Mom was anxious to have us from under her feet for a while, she was reluctant to send us to Great-Aunt Nell Judy's after the time we came home bloomerless.

"What in the name of God could Nell Judy be thinking of?" Mom asked. "Letting you two run around like that! Why didn't you know enough, Beatrice, to insist on wearing your underpants? At eight years old you should know better. Why, Anna, didn't you speak up? That woman is shameless and shiftless. She hasn't a lick of decency. Why, it takes no time at all to wash underwear. I sent you both with two pairs each. Mark my words and mark them well, this is the last time you'll ever go there. I won't have her disgracing me in front of all those people up in the hills."

Daddy was more concerned by the tales we came home with, our terror of the dark, and our nightmares about Great-Uncle Pat. But when Mom and Daddy learned that Beady walked in her sleep there, they both became alarmed. Nevertheless, we were sent time and again. Our fears were overshadowed by our fascination for Great-Aunt Nell Judy's ability to interpret omens. Some said she had second sight because she was born with a caul.

Great-Uncle Pat had been dead for at least ten years when Mom got sick and had to ship Beady and me off to Nell's house. I recall the scene clearly, although I couldn't have been more than six. She was thrilled to have us because we were the perfect audience for her. When she read our palms, Beady and I learned that we both had long life-lines and passionate natures. Beady was going to have seven children and I was going to have "lots of lovers, all dark, Eyetalian types." Beady rubbed her two index fingers at me, the sign language for "shame," and I was inflamed by my prospects. When Great-Aunt Nell Judy rose to start supper, she paused near the big glass bowl on the dresser in the kitchen. Her shiny eyes misted over and she said, "Did you know that Pat walked last night?" Beady and I sat up like rods. My sister's voice stabbed through the silence. "What happened?" she asked.

"Well," Great-Aunt said, "see this bowl? This is where I keep Pat's cuff links, the pair we were married in. Well, he always takes them out and puts them beside the bowl to let me know he's been by. But last night was different. I had gone up to bed, tired from being on my foot the whole day, do you see? As I undid my hair, I heard the pi-anna playing Pat's favorite tune. I came to the head of the stairs. There in the parlor, when I turned on the hall light, I saw the pi-anna stool turning round but there wasn't a soul in sight."

"Well, then, how do you know it was Great-Uncle Pat?" I asked.

My aunt smiled knowingly at Beady, who, though confused, was proud to be her ally. "I know," Great-Aunt said quietly. "Oh, I know!" Her eyes shot heavenward.

For supper she served white buttered bread, lima bean soup, biscuits, and raisin tarts. "Did I ever tell you girls about the time I was locked in church?" she asked afterwards.

"Oh, tell us, Great-Aunt," we begged.

Nell Judy returned to her place at the round table where the oilcloth was worn thin. Gathering up crumbs on her wet finger, she began. "Well, this happened when Pat was still alive. I was just a girl. I didn't have all this old weight on me. I was so little, Pat could practically put his hands around my waist. Anyway, I was quite a churchgoer in those days, and I mind I went to make a novena for my sister Lizzy, who died of sugar diabetes.

"It was November, just before Thanksgiving. I had on the thinnest little coat ever and it was rainy and bitter cold. When I got to the church with all the beautiful candles, it was just so cozy that I dozed off. When I woke up, there wasn't a living soul in the church. The Father had locked up for the night.

"I went to the back doors and they were shut tight as a drum; I even tried the door next to the altar and that was barred to me. I kneeled down before our blessed mother, Queen of the Apostles. As I prayed to her, a hand touched my shoulder. I could tell that it was 'Him.'" She paused and her face grew radiant.

"Who's Him — Uncle Pat?" I asked.

Great-Aunt just shook her head and lowered her eyes. "Our Blessed Savior," she whispered.

"Who, Beady?" I asked in frustration.

"God," Beady flashed in exasperation. "God, dumbbell!" she repeated vehemently.

"Oh," I said. "How could you tell?"

"I saw His halo. He just raised His arm and those big wooden doors opened for me," Great-Aunt answered, smiling. "His presence was the most beautiful thing I've ever known." She looked at me lovingly, and wet her finger in her tiny mouth. "You have grape jelly on your chin, blessed," she said as she rubbed it ever so sweetly, licking her finger like a mother cat. "Now go on up and get into your night clothes."

The next morning we awoke to a gorgeous fall day. The air was tingling clean; the fall leaves fluttered down on the hills. Even the rickety grey steps leading to the weathered wooden houses were brightened by the splash of autumn color.

Great-Aunt Nell Judy greeted us, wearing a man's brown sweater that was worn at the elbows and frayed at the hem around her hips. She pulled at little threads of wool, biting them off, ratlike, with her little teeth. "This was Pat's sweater," she said. "It's getting as old as we are." Then she buttered two thick slices of white bread and coated them with sugar and passed one to Beady and one to me.

"Now you go down hill, Beady, and get me a pound of lard. Tell them to charge it to Mrs. O'Keefe. And Anna, you go down to the cellar for apples. I'm going to make pies today and apple tarts for supper."

The door to the cellar opened like a coffin lid. I remember the strong musty smell coming up from the darkness because the cellar floor was earthen. The apples were in brown sacks near the coal bin. I left the door ajar and the light shot through mercifully, outlining a sharp triangle of light over the sacks. As I bent to pick up the apples, cradling them in my dress front, a shadow passed over the light. I looked up and saw a man smile and then disappear into thin air. My heart sprang to my throat as the apples went flying. I crashed through the screen door. "Great-Aunt Nell Judy!" I screamed. "I just saw Great-Uncle Pat."

My aunt looked at me and then weighed the moment. "Why nonsense," she said. "What would he be doing down there this time of day? That's all in your imagination, honey. He wouldn't be coming to you . . . certainly wouldn't dream of frightening a child. When he went — and it was straight to heaven — more people showed up at his wake than even your grandfather's. No, sweetheart, Pat wouldn't be wandering around at this time of day; and certainly if he frightened you, he'd never forgive himself!"

All the same, I knew I had seen him. To this day, I can tell exactly what he looked like. He was wearing overalls and a brown sweater, old and raggedy, just like the one Great-Aunt Nell Judy had on.

It's little wonder that with all the talk of death and ghosts and Great-Aunt's seeming intimacy with God Himself, I took to imagining things when I was at her house. Although I never saw "Him" as she had, Jesus touched me one night. When he placed his five fingers on my five toes, my throat constricted so that I could not swallow, my heart raced so hard I was sure it would wake my Great-Aunt. I vowed that this would be the last time I'd ever stay alone with her in her house.

Nell Judy was surrounded by the aura of mysteries and seemed to attract disaster. The house and the hills around it were haunted. Even the tree with the swing had a scary association.

The summer just before my seventh birthday, I was sent to visit because Beady had chicken pox and Mom had her hands full. Great-Aunt always welcomed me because she said I was good company and could run errands for her. Though Beady was bigger and could do more, I could stand on a box and hang her wash. On that visit I learned that something had happened to Dennis Duffy, the boy who usually did chores for her. It was a horrid tale, which I never got quite straight because Aunt Nell Judy told it with looks and whispers. Whatever she said made Daddy reluctant to leave me there, but Great-Aunt insisted that it was for the best. She kept pleading, "Oh John, with Duffy gone, she's a godsend."

Some time later I learned that Dennis was accidentally killed while playing war with some other boys who had caught him and hanged him for desertion, all in sport. Beady and I both remembered him: he was thirteen, tall and skinny, and could walk on thistles without shoes, climb trees, and jump from high places. He went after birds with his bean shooter, so we didn't like him much. But after he got hanged, we felt sorry and guilty about him.

On the day I came with my father, I overheard him ask my aunt, "Where did it happen?" And Great-Aunt answered, "Near the big oak."

After Daddy left, I got restless and lonesome and kept banging in and out of the screen door. Great-Aunt was sitting with her sore leg resting on a chair, mixing dough for raisin muffins. I helped her by chasing flies, but soon tired of slapping around with the fly swatter.

"Why don't you go on out up the steps and play on the rope swing? Maybe some other girl will see you and play too," Great-Aunt suggested. Rickety wooden steps wended their way all through those hills near her house. The swing hung on the branch of a big oak tree and you could swing downhill on it. It sent chilly thrills right up through my underpants and set me giggling gaily, head thrown back in the wind and eyes skyward.

I had to pump myself along because there was no one to push me. I had at last achieved some speed when suddenly the sky went dark and the wind raised clouds of dust and tore the leaves from trembling branches. My swing twirled crazily. I jumped off, banging my back on the seat board, and fell down in pain, the breath knocked out of me. As I was spitting on my scraped palm and bleeding knee, I heard laughter. It was an eerie sound in the strange light and lull that comes before a summer storm; everything became perfectly still. I saw four shapes—all smaller than midgets, little men, knee-high. They held hands in ring-around-the-rosy and kicked up their legs and danced. I let out a blood-curdling scream. As I skidded down the last flight of steps to my aunt's front porch, she pushed open the screen door with hands covered in dough. "Why my God in heaven, what's the matter?" she asked.

My hard breathing made my chest ache. I swallowed, trying to compose myself, because what I had to tell was so important. I drew out my tale to give it exaggerated weight. "Guess what," I asked. "Guess what I saw while I was play-ing at the swing."

"What?" my aunt asked.

"I saw four little men dancing and laughing on the hill."

A frown creased her brow. She took even longer than I had to speak. "Where were they dancing?" she asked, a note of concern creeping into her voice.

"Where the grass is worn off. Near the swing."

"Uh-huh," she said, "by the big oak . . ." and then she stopped herself. Great-Aunt looked up at the sky and continued, her voice low and ominous, "Well come on inside. That's a sure sign of rain. We're going to have an awful downpour." I saw her glance back up the hill and I thought I saw her shudder. I interpreted her look and her prediction to mean she was reading an omen from the event.

She was right. It poured; the rainbarrel flooded; the tar roof leaked. I tried looking through the rain-streaked window up the hill toward the swing, but the little men, the Faeries, were gone. I never saw them again.

The move from Tarentum to Job's Hole in the fall of 1931 devastated my mother. The tiny valley inhabited by poor whites and poor blacks was not her idea of a fit place to live. The miners and mill hands who would be our neighbors lived in makeshift, run-down shacks with tin-fluted roofs and sagging wooden porches. The fencing was made from discarded bedsprings that had rusted in the rain.

Not only was Job's Hole across the tracks, but it was tucked away from the town of Tarentum and hidden in the back hills. It was accessible by bus if you could survive the ride. The turnoff wasn't marked, but it was the dirt road just beyond Dead Man's Curve.

Though our new house sat primly on a hill overlooking the valley, it was a frightful comedown. We had acres of land for Pop to plant, but only four small rooms to live in.

On the morning we moved in, Daddy plunked us on the Polaski porch, while he and our new neighbor, Mr. Polaski, went up the hill to set up the heavy furniture. As I looked up from the valley, I grew excited at the prospect of exploring my new environs. I saw an expanse of rolling grassy upland, and to the right of our new home, a forest of young trees, all golden and crimson. I watched Mom defoliate them with a glance. She knew only too well how dismal the winter would be.

She sat stiffly on the wicker swing, wearing her best navy dress, matching cloche, and gloves. In fact, we were all dressed to the nines in her favorite color, navy blue, which she said was "refined." Katherine huddled close to her, wearing her good sailor blouse and pleated skirt. Beady and I wore hats and our Sunday shoes.

The Polaskis had hordes of half-clad, tow-headed children chasing in and out of side doors and jumping up and down the porch steps. Their house was the roomiest in the valley, built by Mr. Polaski with his own hands. His wife, whose name sounded like "Lawusha," assured Mom that Bussie, her husband, would "help us any way he could." Lawusha was fat and jolly and not Mom's type at all. She sat squeezed in her rocker in a dress so tight that it hiked up, exposing her fat dimpled knees and huge thighs.

When she tugged out her breast and began feeding her baby in front of us, I thought my mother would go through the porch floor. Her face, already flushed from the excitement, went beet red. Beady and I met each other's glance, fascinated by Mrs. Polaski and her blue-veined titty. When she finished feeding the infant, she hauled up a big two-year-old and nursed it as well.

We had never witnessed such a phenomenon before and, as Mom could have predicted, it went right into our bag of tricks. Mom knew just where to trace our behavior when she caught us undoing the straps of our sundresses and hugging our baby dolls to our chests. To her everlasting shame and chagrin, when Mrs. Polaski was pregnant again we shoved pillows up our dresses and walked around the yard, shocking the neighbors. Job's Hole was to become an inferno for my mother. She sensed it from the first.

That first night it got dark and gloom set in. We all sat around the kitchen table wearing our coats and hats. Pop brought a kerosene lamp and soup up from the Polaskis', but Mom wouldn't touch a morsel of food. She kept her purse in her lap, took out her hanky, and cried.

"I'm not staying in this hovel, John. Why, I can't believe what you've done to us. When we drove into this hellhole today and I saw all those colored people . . . and Katherine a young lady. Why, my God in heaven, there's no telling what those colored men will try to do to her.

"And Mrs. Polaski sitting on her porch like that, exposing herself, with those miners passing by and her just nodding and waving to them. I was embarrassed to tears.

"How in the world," she continued, "am I going to get to the store with my milk leg over that awful cinder road and down that dirt hill in front of us? I'm taking the train home to Ma'am's a' Monday and I'm taking Anna with me."

"No, you go yourself, Stella. They are not missing school because of your foolishness." Pop slammed the door for emphasis.

Mom looked around at the kitchen, at the pump on the sink, and at the galvanized bucket. There was the big iron stove, which would need tending and lugging of fuel. The smelly kerosene lamp threw a dim light onto the wooden barrels in the middle of the room. Mom's shadow shot up the side of the walls and bent into the ceiling. "Where in the world," she cried, "will I have room for all my nice things?"

"I'll have to keep my china cupboard shoved in a

corner of that front room for no one to see. All my parlor furniture and my mahogany dining room table will have to be crowded in there as well. There's not a bit of room for my relatives to come. I'll just have to sleep them in that crowded parlor. I'll die of shame here, Katherine . . . I really will."

"Well, Mom, it's not the parlor that's so awful," Katherine said; "it's that hideous outhouse."

Mom burst into fresh sobs at the mention of this. She stormed over to the sink and noisily pumped water into a bucket. "We'll leave this in your room near the beds. We can't be doing our business up there in the pitch dark. You girls will just have to go in the bucket, and tomorrow when it's light, we'll figure a way. Oh my God, children." Mom's voice cracked again. "I'll never forgive your father for this. Never."

We had our first Sunday in Job's Hole. Pop did fall gardening while Mom and Katherine prepared the chicken. Beady polished her money and hid it in a baking powder can. I went out and stood in the yard. While I was studying the little bugs floating in the water of the rain barrel, a girl ventured into our yard and watched me from the foot of our hill. When she caught my eye, she smiled, put her arms behind her back, and climbed up toward me. As she approached, she extended a hand, unclenched her fist, and presented me with a butternut. I noticed something funny about her. Her light brown hair was frizzy and her eyes so green they looked like the insides of grapes. Her skin was the color of tea with milk in it.

"My name's Bonnie," she said in a voice deep and hoarse. But when she giggled, it was high-pitched, and when she muffled it with her little grubby hands, I noticed that she bit her nails, too. I liked her right away and invited her to sit on my porch swing.

I saw my father climb higher on the hill near the outhouse, his rake slung over his shoulder. Whistling a Croatian song, he threw me a glance and winked.

Bonnie and I jabbered away, anxious to get through the preliminaries. I learned that she was going on seven and her last name was Stewart. Her cousin Alice lived down the hill next to the Polaskis. Her father was a miner.

"Oh, my grandfather was a miner," I said excitedly. I wanted to have something in common with her. I was still in my shy period, but I blabbed away to Bonnie about Grandpa, Uncle Vincent, Uncle Jim, and the mines in Scotchville, until Mom summoned me into the kitchen.

"Come over here to me, Lady Jane," Mom ordered and lowered her voice a mite. "I don't want you telling that colored girl your business. You tell her you have to stay in to eat."

When I pushed open the screen door, Bonnie had heard my mother's words and fled. I plopped onto a kitchen chair and sulked.

"Put your dress down, Anna, and sit up. I don't like indolence, you know. Honest to God, I don't know where you get your notions. Your grandfather, Lady Jane, was no ordinary miner. He was a fire boss and he inspected those mines, because if there were any leaks, those miners would be blown to bits. Pap had an important job and don't you forget it. He never drank or smoked a day in his life, my father."

"But he chewed tobacco, Mom," I argued. I didn't like my mother's "better than" attitude and I didn't like her saying "*my* father" like that. She seemed to be one-upping me.

"Grandma even says that Pap chewed, because Uncle Vincent and Uncle Jimmy use Pap's old spittoon."

At the mention of Pap's spittoon, her eyes welled up.

"Here, get my clean hanky in my purse," she said pointing toward her room. "All men who go into mines have to chew to keep their throats moist because of the awful coal dust. He raised all of us nine children and worked right up till his death. Your grandfather was seventy-six when God took him. Well," Mom said, standing up, "your father will be wanting his meal soon, so I better get the table set. I'm grateful for one thing, though, that Pap never lived to see us in this awful place."

Job's Hole, I know, is an awful sounding name to wax sentimental about, but the memories both pleasant and unpleasant have a fierce hold on me, maybe because they are all firsts. I caught my first butterfly there, creeping up to the flower where it lit, waiting for the second when it raised all four wings and dug its antennae into the heart of a flower before I pinched it. Its desperate flutter felt like a scream for freedom and I let go, but the stain of yellow powder on my fingers filled me with sickening guilt because Beady told me that once you touch the powdered wings you might as well keep the butterfly in a jar; it will die anyway.

And Job's Hole was where I first got lobster red from the hot sun and Mom forced me to wear a sunbonnet. But freckles be damned, sunburn or blisters, nothing could keep me from swimming in the river off Bull Creek Road. I would never become a swimming champion — Eleanor Holm and Esther Williams were destined for that. I used to go alone and thrash about in the water imitating the older kids until one time I was porpoise diving and one of the older black boys goosed me. I was too shocked and ashamed to fight him on it. I left the river in tears and ran home to suffer chills and sunburn. From then on I only waded in the creek or cooled off under the drain on the roof. As a result, I can't swim.

Job's Hole is where I first started school.

I was devastated when Daddy took me the first day and I was rejected because I didn't have my vaccination. It wasn't until the end of September, almost a month late, before I could start the first grade. Katherine and Beatrice had gotten new shoes, clothes, books and pencil cases for school, but I was low on the priority list and always got my things last. By the time I had my vaccination scab, my serge skirt was pressed with a damp cloth, Daddy'd bought me a new pencil box, and my turn came to go to school at last, I was near hysteria.

The evening before I was going to finally leave my mother at home and go to school, I laid out my clothes and polished my new oxfords again and again. In a fit of exasperation, Mom told Katherine to "take that polish away from her or she'll rub the leather bare."

That night I tossed and turned and went on the bucket so many times during the night that I woke the whole house up. "Get her to stop, Mom," my sisters screamed out in unison. "Why do we have to have the Runt in the room with us? We can't sleep with her prowling about."

Daddy stirred and cursed in his sleep. To pacify him, Mom said groggily, "If your father has to come in to you girls, you'll know it!" That must have quieted me down, because I didn't dare budge or noise about until dawn when Mom got up to start the coal stove. The oatmeal was soaked and made the night before, so it just needed to be warmed up. As soon as I heard her at the stove shaking the ashes, I flew to her side. I pulled the kitchen chair over and Mom whispered in her early morning voice. "Go put your carpet slippers on. This floor's cold and I haven't scrubbed it yet."

I kept my voice to a whisper too. "I hope I like my teacher, don't you, Mamma? Beady hates hers. Beady says mine's very mean, too. She hits the children, Beady says."

Mom placed the sugar bowl on the table. "Don't be going on about what Beady says. She likes to scare you. Go in and get dressed; then you can help me set the table. We'll need the big spoons," Mom said when I returned. "Give Beady the sugar spoon — the one embossed with roses . . . not the plain one; she won't eat with that."

"Couldn't I have the rose one this morning since it's my turn?" I asked.

"Oh my God," Mom whispered in alarm. "Don't cross her this morning, or there will be the devil to pay. She's a bear when she gets up; and God knows I've had enough trouble without having that tyrant on me. Just give it to her to keep the peace."

Peace was not kept for long because as soon as Beady entered the scene, she started. "I can't find my school dress, Mom."

"It's hanging on the door hook. I ironed it like you asked," Mom said.

"Why is the Runt sitting in my place?"

I had placed my chair next to my father's. "Mom said I could sit here in the new house," I argued. "The sugar spoon is at your place, Beady, even though it's my turn."

"I want you near me, anyway, Beatrice," Mom said.

"Okey doke, but I'm sitting there for supper, Runt, and don't forget it."

"Eat your oats and stop bickering," Mom poured some sugar into the bowl and warned me about using too much or "you'll get sugar diabetes like my Aunt Lizzy. That's how she died, poor thing. Save some milk for the others, Beady. You're drowning those oats."

At eight o'clock Daddy and Katherine headed for Tarentum. Mom hurried me out the door to catch the school bus, which Beady flatly refused to take. "I'll go with her if she walks, but I'm not riding that bus," she said, and headed for the shortcut over the creek and up the hill near the spring.

I met Bonnie Stewart coming down the cinder path.

She took my hand and we tore down the dirt hill together to catch the bus in front of the country store on Bull Creek Road. Bonnie sat close to me, whispering the names of all the other children, who looked so dark and strange to me. We joggled along the bus route on our way to Natrona Heights, circling the wooded hills and grassy vales. Just before we got to where the houses were expensive and nice, the driver turned sharply and halted near a shabby schoolhouse in the middle of barren fields. Bonnie jumped up and got off with all the black kids. She waved and smiled at me, then I saw her fling her arm around the neck of a little black girl and they danced into step with each other. I was left with only three other white kids on that bus, and we averted our eyes and gazed out the windows as the bus driver whirled the bus around and hauled us off to our school. We passed pretty green lawns and whitewashed fences with neatly paved sidewalks and "Christ Saves" churches. At the end of the ride, in bucolic splendor, sat our school, heavy green ivy climbing up the red brick walls.

Miss Hardy, the first grade teacher, frizzed her hair with a curling iron. She was skinny and her stocking seams curved up her bony legs. Very strict and cranky, she was rattled by the least bit of noise. If a child dropped a book she'd jump and act annoyed. When Miss Hardy caught me biting my nails, she scolded me in front of the whole class. Afterwards, Charles Edwards, who sat next to me, leaned over and whispered in my ear, "Miss Hardy has a wart on her nose because she touched a frog." His tongue was milk-coated and his breath smelled of farina. He crinkled his freckled nose when he laughed. I fell in love with Charles during that first week in school and we sent love notes to each other as soon as we learned to print.

I made friends with Charlotte Jean Miller because she lived near Charles, so I walked her home every day in order to be near him. I kept missing the school bus and had to suffer scoldings from my mother for dallying after school. Sometimes the sun fell before I was ready to go home and I had to make my way through the dark woods, my heart in my mouth. Once I reached the safety of the clearing, however, I would review everything Charles had said and done and I would feel ecstatically happy. As Great-Aunt Nell Judy had predicted, Charles was dark with brown eyes. Starting with him, all my lovers fit that description.

All through that first autumn in Jobsey, except for rainy days, I followed Beady and walked to school. The bus had little appeal for me. I learned to balance my books and run across the narrow board that spanned the river. It led to the shortcut, a winding path through the woods carpeted with red and yellow leaves. Just before we reached the incline, we usually stopped at the spring for a drink. Once out of the woods, we walked on pavement, skipping cracks, racing to beat the bus, which we usually did.

But as winter set in, the shortcut became impractical

and I joined the bus brigade again with Bonnie. Mom cut down Aunt Gert's old brown wraparound coat for me and I jammed my wool tam down over my ears. The ground tightened and froze; the bridge plank iced over and became slippery, as did the hills. Even the steel clasps on my garter supporters grew icy. The skinny trees were naked grey sticks, silhouetting their black, fragile branches against grey sky. Our cherry tree, too, became a drab skeleton leaning over the garage roof. The birds' nests, vacated now, blew apart in the wind. All the shacks' chimneys coughed out black coal smoke, and ash piles formed at the sides of houses. It would be a long time before those ashes fed the pansy beds.

I looked forward to huddling on the bus with the black kids, but Beady could never adjust to that. She said she was looked down on by her classmates because she lived in Job's Hole. She felt her teacher shamed her into feeling inferior. These feelings persisted in spite of the fact that she was the best dressed of the Jackson girls, having inherited the outgrown clothing of our rich cousins.

Beady developed a hatred for school that grew into an obsession. She began feigning illnesses that kept her at home for days on end. Mom ran herself to a frazzle tending to Beady's "illnesses": heating oil for an earache, dispensing paregoric for a stomachache, winding a flannel around a sore throat. The Vicks salve smelled throughout the house, and even seeped onto the handle of the big wooden spoon Mom used to ladle up the rolled oats. Beady would send her back to the kitchen for more sugar for the porridge, more milk, or more weak tea. She usually would wait till Dad had left for work before making her demands, because Daddy was wise to her tricks and would get furious at Mom for "indulging the Beatrice like this." But Mom argued that Beady was delicate and needed her care.

On the morning Beady changed her dress for the third time, the big fight occurred. With foot stamping and hand hipping, she rejected my mother's plea that she wear a certain frock. The blue dress she wanted to wear was outside frozen on the line.

"You'll be late for school, honey," my mother pleaded. "Wear your green dress, for my sake, Beady. That was Cousin Vera's. Why, Aunt Anne made that dress and it's just beautiful."

"No, I hate it," Beady said, standing impudently in her undershirt and bloomers. Her cotton stockings were pulled taut on her skinny legs. Even at nine years old Beady was very fussy about baggy knees.

"Well, then, wear your navy skirt and white waist and I'll iron your blue dress tonight," Mother again pleaded.

"The white blouse has a big ink stain and I hate that old skirt." Beady squinted her eyes at Mom and challenged her on to the next argument. Her pleasure at rejecting suggestions mounted until my father pushed aside his egg plate, tore off his glasses, and lunged toward Beady in a fury.

"Goddamn it, Beatrice, do as the mother says."

"Don't be cursing, Daddy; don't be taking the Lord's name in vain," Mom said.

"Come in here, Beatrice," Daddy commanded, pointing to a seam on the linoleum floor. "Stand here." It was a command that was always obeyed. We stood exactly on that seam and were either slapped or dosed with castor oil by our father, according to the situation. It was unthinkable to defy him; we didn't even dare raise our hands in reflex to ward off a blow.

But Beady, in her underwear, rebelled. She fled to the

parlor and used the round, mahogany table as a barricade. Her blue eyes flashed, her nostrils flared. Beads of excited perspiration separated her bangs.

My father positioned himself opposite her. The two combatants waited to see who would move first. If Daddy chased her to the right, Beady ran to the left, balancing her hands on the table and anticipating his next move. Katherine, Mom, and I watched from the sidelines. When my mother grabbed for Daddy's arm, he jerked it away with a suddenness that sent her reeling. "Son a mum bitch, keep out of this, Stella," he warned. "Beatrice, you will pay for this. I'm warning you once more. You wear that goddamned clothing . . ."

"Oh please, don't swear, John. Oh, I beg of you on my mercy. I'll iron the blue dress. I'll bring it from the line."

"Stay where you are, Stella," Daddy threatened. "No ironing." Now he pointed once more to his spot. "Beatrice, come in here," he ordered, his voice now reaching a crescendo.

Beady placed her hands on her hips and, matching volume and fury, said, "I won't come. I refuse to be beaten by you. I don't care if you kill me." The chase started again, around and around, and then the dance from side to side. Suddenly our father stopped. He lowered his head and shook it. We heard wheezing gasps which sounded as if he was crying.

To our astonishment we discovered that he was trying to suppress his laughter. He wiped his eyes, replaced his glasses, and threw back his head. "Oh God my," he kept saying between fits of uncontrollable bursts of laughter. "I have to admire that spirit. She's father's daughter, all right."

Beady was left in a state of confusion. She was not at all sure that it was safe to leave her place, for Daddy could trick you into thinking his mood had changed. But this morning it was genuine. Mom finally got Beady to put on the blue skirt and to wear a jersey top by promising that she'd soak the ink stain in milk and then bleach it with lemon juice.

Daddy tidied his hair at the kitchen sink. He was mumbling to himself as he left for work. He stopped on the icy path near the garage, hunching his shoulders to ward off the cold. A shiver went through him as the chill of the morning attacked . . . or maybe it was a recall of laughter. At any rate, he quickened his pace, shook his head in amused disbelief, revved the engine of his Ford and motored down the cinder path toward his Scientific Beauty Shop in Tarentum.

Once we were settled in Job's Hole, I rarely was taken into Tarentum to my dad's shop. Katherine drove into town with him daily and folded towels there after school. Beady got a fingerwave on a Saturday as a reward for going to the doctor's office and having her carbuncle lanced; but I had not reached the age of vanity, so it was torture enduring Dad's beautifying sessions at home.

Every Sunday after Dad's gardening, all of us, including Mom, had to have our hair cut and fingerwaved because my father said, "When you go out, you are walking advertisement for my trade." After these hair sessions, Dad lined us up in the yard in front of or between his rows of yellow coreopsis and while we squinted in the sunlight he snapped our picture. Not a photo exists of me or my mother with our eyes open, but Daddy's handiwork is recorded by Kodak for all time. Our hair is glued to our heads in a series of undulating waves with a curl like a ringworm plastered on our cheeks.

The first time I visited the shop Daddy began priming me for the Demonstration. He explained carefully that I was going to be "the chosen one. We are going to display new scientific wonder in shop window on a Saturday and people are going to see me give you the first permanent wave. You know, daughts, like the Lindbergh who was first to cross Atlantic, this experiment is going to prove big accomplishment you can boast about."

Inwardly, I was excited about being the "one" for this special demonstration, since I wouldn't have to sit like Mom and Katherine and Beady for a set every Sunday.

The day before the big event, my mother had me try on a silk dress Beatrice had outgrown. She shortened it by tucking it up at the waist. It had a flared green skirt attached to a white, sleeveless vee-necked bodice and a green silk jacket with long, fitted sleeves and a tiny button at each wrist. It was the most grownup dress I'd ever had.

Beady screamed when she saw Mom fitting it to me. "That's my dress! Cousin Vera gave it to me! I don't want the Runt to have it."

"Now, Beady," Mom said, "be a good girl and I'll tell you what. I'll send for some silk and make you a dress just like this one. And I'll give you a nickel for your bank if you stop this hollering."

"If I give up my best and only silk dress," Beady bargained, "I'll have to have more than an old nickel because I'll be saving up for myself. I have to have at least a quarter."

Beady slipped an I.O.U. into her baking powder can and the issue of the dress was settled after much wrangling, Beady having outfoxed my mother once more.

I was already up that Saturday morning when my father, shivering in his undershirt, danced over the cold kitchen floor. "Well, well, well," he said, "look who's first one out the bed."

I sat in my flannel nightgown on a kitchen chair with my knees held close to my body and tucked my nightgown under my feet to keep warm.

"It's chilly morning, huh?" said Dad. "I hope sun is going to come out because folks are going to be looking at you in shop window."

He went over to the window and peered out. "Well, we can only hope for best."

Mom fried cornmeal mush and spread mine with apple butter. I ate in my nightgown so my dress wouldn't get soiled. My Mary Janes were shined with Vaseline, and Mom had to pin my slip up on the shoulder because it hung below my dress on one side.

I was excited and proud to be going into Tarentum with my father. The dew was still on the grass when we started down the hill. Daddy had made a stone path on the side of the hill where his baby's breath and ageratum grew. There was just the barest suggestion of spring now, though Daddy checked as we walked, tut-tutting and sniffing the air. "Watch you don't step on earth there, Anna. Keep on steps. I have all kinds surprises over there. You know, not long now they will be pulled by sun from their dark hiding places."

When we arrived at Dad's shop, the Scientific Beauty Parlor, I got my first glimpse of the permanent wave machine in the window. It was a huge apparatus, with corkscrew-like tubes attached to wires which hung on a big iron pole. There was a high stool for me to sit on. A kid had been hired to give out flyers for the demonstration, which was starting at eleven-thirty. My being the guinea pig was meant to prove that even a child of six could have a wave and not be scared by the harmless apparatus.

When the tinfoil and the corkscrews were attached, and the hot, heavy, and hideous curlers yanked my hair hard from the roots, I became apprehensive. Women, men, and children were staring in at me and I began to snivel. Pop scurried around me, whispering reassurances before he scolded me.

"God damn it, daughts, stop this bawling. Those people think you being murdered. You know, you supposed to be good example for the machine." The torture went on for hours. The relief of finally being unwired was overwhelming. I was clapping my shoes together in anticipation, waiting to see my gorgeous curls.

Pop, looking very businesslike, examined each frizz of hair and tugged at it to show the people that it didn't fall out. I then had to have water combed through to demonstrate its lasting effects.

Waves were fingered into place. The ends were encouraged to defy gravity and flip up over my ears. I was brought a hand mirror and my face lit up. I remember smiling faces, people applauding, and a small girl resting one foot on the other. For no reason at all, she touched her thumb to her nose and stuck out her tongue. I wanted to grimace back at her, but I was confused and I could feel my face burn and my throat tighten so I lowered my eyes.

"Old mean rat face," I said to myself. "I don't care what she thinks." Pop lifted me off the stool, smiled and waved to the dispersing crowd.

When they had gone, he went behind the screen to wash up. I twirled around, making my dress flare. I looked at myself in the mirrored wall. I went up so close that my breath fogged the mirror and I pressed my lips and nose in the glass and kissed my own reflection.

Beady was insanely jealous of my curls, so Mom set her hair in rags and to further pacify her gave her a pair of white curtains to use for dress-up. With one panel pinned to her head and the other used as a skirt, we marched off to play in the rabbit coop. I danced attendance on her by making sure her train did not get caught on the ladder that led up to our little house on stilts.

And then one night Daddy brought home Bunny Girl, pregnant, and presented her to Beady and me, "so you and your sister will learn about birth and life," Dad said as he handed Bunny Girl to Beady.

He instructed us carefully on the do's and don't's of rabbit owning. First off, there would be no more playing in the coop. "Now is home of rabbit." He told us to pick plantain leaves. "That's what rabbit likes to eat; you can also give piece of carrot." We were told to change the water daily and to "Give little salt — and collect turds. Perfect fertilizer as is pure alfalfa. No smell because she's wegetarian, not carnivorous like we are." The turds went right into Daddy's rock garden of velvet blue and yellow pansies. My sister and I ran through the paths of coreopsis, a hardy flower for which Pop won a blue ribbon, but we were warned never to tramp near the pansy bed.

One rainy Saturday Bunny Girl gave birth to babies galore. Beady and I stood in the drizzling rain with our skirts hiked up over our heads gaping in amazement at her litter of little pink-skinned, closed-eyed, ratty things.

When they grew hair, Daddy supervised a winnowing out. We could have "a brother and a sister. You can call them Jack and Jill," Pop said, "and of course, we'll keep the mother." The rest of the litter went back to the farmer and Daddy hinted at their fate. Bunny Girl had grown too fat and nervous to fondle. Her pink nose was forever twitching above her hare lip. Jack and Jill, however, were huggable and livelier. Beady and I loved fondling them and were constantly pulling them out of the coop and letting them chase about in the yard.

I'll say this for Mom: she warned us. "Don't, for God's sake, be letting those things run loose, or there'll be hell to pay when your father comes home. I'm warning you two."

Disobeying Mom, we let the rabbits out to run about, so we could climb up into the shade of the coop, where I served Queen Beatrix "tea" in her little tin cup. When we finished playing there we returned Bunny Girl, who had just sat like a lump near the steps, quivering. Jill was cooling herself under the porch steps and wouldn't come out. I had to belly-whop under the breezeway and scare her toward Beady. Jack was nowhere in sight. We looked high and low and as night approached fear and guilt set in. Mom just shook her head in dismay. "Oh my God, girls; I don't know what your father will say. . . . I warned you. . . ."

We begged Mom not to tell and she kept her word, but when we were having supper that night, a dog came chasing up our hill barking ferociously. With a wad of food stuck in his cheek, Pop pushed open the screen door in time to see Jack leap onto the porch swing. Daddy threw a broom at the dog to shoo him off. My sister and I held our breath while Daddy tended to the fracas. When he returned, he stood in the doorway shaking his head hopelessly.

"Oh, God my," he said mournfully. "Why did you let rabbit out? He died of fright, poor thing." Beady left the table crying. Mom and Kay went after her and I went to the screen door and saw my father take the shovel up the hill to dig a grave. Poor Beady was inconsolable for days.

Pop brought us another rabbit, which Beady and I didn't take to at all. Then we reverted to our old ways of lugging him around and letting him frolic about. Pop came home one night to find his ravaged pansy bed eaten to the nub. Resolute, he taught us a lesson we will never forget.

In grim determination, he headed for the rabbit coop, grabbed the new rabbit by the scruff of the neck, gave it a quick and expert yank and then informed Mom that we'd be having stewed rabbit for supper that night. He returned Bunny Girl and Jill to the farmer. Mom would not speak to Pop for days after this, and Beady and I cried ourselves to sleep at night.

Months, or maybe even a year later, the subject came up out of the blue one night. Dad came home bleary-eyed. He loosened his tie, ran his hand through his thinning blond hair, removed his tortoise-shell glasses, buried his face in his hands, and cried. My mother stormed out of the kitchen, having already ladled his food on his plate. My sister and I started to sneak out, but my father stopped us.

"No, no, no! Anna, Beatrice, sit. Sit a minute, girls. I want to explain to you something. The mother thinks I don't know what I'm doing. I know why I cry. It is from the soul. You remember? Oh, God my, it hurts me so to say it. You remember that time with the Bunny Girl? You remember why that happened? I know, I know; you don't forgive me for that. . . . I don't forgive myself for that . . . but it was not something I could control.

"I *warned*. I said '*Never, never* let the rabbits out of the coop again.' You remember that, Beatrice? You remember that, Anna? I warned you. I begged you. You did it time and time again. The one little rabbit got chased by the dog . . . you remember that . . . and died stiff on the swing. How sweet I was . . . I buried that rabbit for you. But when you deceived me, when you wouldn't listen to the father, when you didn't respect me, that's when I did it.

"You think it was easy to eat that Goddamned rabbit. No, it was not easy! I was choking on every bite. How do you think sensitive human being feels who has to do such a thing? But I had to teach you girls . . . I had to let you know that when the father makes request, when the father makes rules, he must be obeyed. When he asks for the discipline, he must get it. If he doesn't get it, then he must punish offenders in whatever way he knows how . . . that was only way I knew how.

"Only way to teach you was what I did . . . something so drastic, to make you understand how much the rabbit mean to you.

"All right, you can go in room with the mother and cry with her. I don't want to see you in here anymore.

"Go on. Go on."

The rabbit coop was empty now, so Beady and I swept out the turds and dried plantain leaves, took out the water dish, and proceeded to convert the coop back to a playhouse. But it was never the same, and we looked about for other things to do. Although Beady and I were forced together, we genuinely enjoyed each other's company, even when she grew bossy and I became passive and saintly. I was constantly giving my candy away, holding out an open palm with my offering, and Beady was usually on the grabbing end. The more I gave the more she took advantage of me. I would always let her go first in our games and I would promise her anything if she agreed to play house with me. Often when she had cleaned me out, I would have second thoughts and would sit martyred and silently suffering my impoverished fate.

This drove Katherine wild. She constantly came to my defense. "You do that to her again, Beady, and I'm not only telling Daddy, but I'll make certain he hears about everything you've done to her. Now give her back her tin cup," or marbles, or doll's dress, or bug jar, or whatever. We would resolve our differences and Beady would throw her arm around my neck and sing,

> *"We're glue,*
> *We're glue,*
> *We're always sticking together."*

Katherine, often having brought about the reconciliation, would invent a game for all three of us. Whenever she deigned to participate in our games, we were ecstatic. She united us in a spirit of camaraderie, and that enthralled us.

Katherine was always dramatic and extremely interested in movies, poetry, and literature. She loved reading aloud and we were a very responsive audience. One spring day, she climbed the hill to the rope swing where Beady and I were playing. We dropped our bug jars and ran to greet her. We had spotted the book she was carrying and were tickled with anticipation and excitement. She settled on a rock in the shade and read us Katherine Mansfield's "The Doll's House," the first short story we had ever heard. Beady and I both loved it and requested it every chance we got. Katherine always complied.

Sometimes she'd read to us in the kitchen after supper. Of the volumes of literature Daddy had supplied us with, the small blue soft-covered books of the *World's Great Stories* series were the ones we liked best. Mom, too, loved to hear Katherine read, and although I don't remember Daddy joining us in the kitchen, he had a pleased look on his face if he chanced upon one of Katherine's sessions. No matter how many times we heard Katherine Mansfield's "The Doll's House," we cried at the description of the poor Kelvy children. My sister extracted every bit of pathos out of those characters. We all knew the story by heart and almost by reflex we chorused the last line with her: "I seen the little lamp." We loved Lil Kelvy and "Our Else" with all our hearts.

Katherine became mentor and stage mother to me. She stood me up on Mom's hope chest, having dressed me in a lace tunic, a piece of finery Mom had been given years before by a wealthy relative. My mother never reprimanded Katherine for taking her things, but if Beady or I dared to open the hope chest, all hell broke loose. Katherine costumed me, rouged my cheeks, and taught me to sing, "I'm a Dreamer, Aren't We All?" with hand motions. I won my mother's approval even though I was "painted" and clad in her good lace. I don't remember experiencing any great excitement or discomfort when I sang, but I can't for the life of me figure out why Katherine chose to teach me songs, since neither she nor I could carry a tune. Beady was a veritable nightingale. Both my and Katherine's specialty was reciting, and my choice and interpretation of poems was determined by my older sister.

I became fascinated by the movies from overhearing Katherine describe to Mom the ones she had seen. Sometimes I was even allowed, if I washed my hands well, to look at Katherine's movie scrapbook. "Greta Garbo's gown was done by Adrian," said Katherine. "Adrian was married to Janet Gaynor. Adrian did all of Joan Crawford's clothes, too." When Katherine saw *Letty Lynton,* she adopted a new image for herself. Joan Crawford must have worn a skullcap in the movie, because my sister cut up my mother's cloche and made herself one just like it. It was never off her head. She wore it to school, to the movies, and to Pop's shop.

One day she involved Beady and me in reenacting *Letty Lynton* outdoors by the garage. She wore her cloche and added Mom's grey fox fur to complete the costume. Beady was cast as the South American lover, played in the movie by Nils Asther. He was the villain of the piece. Letty poisoned him by mistake because he was going to compromise her. She really had meant to kill herself rather than succumb to his advances, but he exchanged glasses with her, drank her champagne, and died. Beady loved playing that dying scene. She acted debonair as she guzzled her root beer, then clutched her throat and coughed and staggered about. She gave Letty one tragic, wounded look before she expired on the ground near the crabapple tree. Just before dropping dead, she checked the stones on the ground to make sure she fell clear of them. Then she threw her body down to earth in her "drop dead" pose . . . her arms outstretched, her summer pajamas falling off one shoulder, her blue eyes open and staring. She always died with her eyes open. Even when she scratched her itchy nose with her fist, her eyes never lost their glazed look. I was to imitate it time and again.

Katherine dropped to her knees and pretended to weep, "Emile, it wasn't meant for you." I remember feeling a sympathetic sob growing in my throat. She was better than Crawford, better than Garbo, better than Kay Francis, even. Katherine was the Duse-Bernhardt of our family.

My first acting part was impersonating Robert Montgomery, the dull good guy in the movie. I wore my father's fedora. It didn't seem to matter to Katherine that I was not much taller than her waist and a girl, so intense was her concentration. Her imagination transformed me into a strong, handsome man, and I grew bold in her belief. I swaggered and rendered Robert Montgomery far more dashing than he ever could have been in his own wildest dreams. Though my caresses were awkward — I could only get my arms around her waist — Katherine would nonetheless be coy and flirtatious with me. The trial scene bored me, so my mind wandered off into a daydream while Katherine acted her heart out. My scene came up after she was acquitted.

We stepped onto the garage roof, pretending it was an ocean liner. The crabapple tree had rained its blossoms on that black tar roof in spring, and now in autumn the little green apples fell in twos, joined at the stem. Katherine hung them over her ears for earrings. A breeze tugged at her red shoulder-length hair, held loosely under her skullcap. She used Pop's Bandoline to make a spit curl at the ear lobe.

"Oh, darling!" she said, as I swaggered beside her to the front of the roof facing the valley where the poor coal miners lived. "Oh, darling," she repeated and she placed her gloved hand on my shoulder. "We'll forget all this when we get to Paris. I'll make you a good wife . . ." her voice broke in a sob.

Then in her normal voice she directed, "Now you must say, 'There, there, Letty. Emile is gone.' Say it," she commanded.

I said it. She listened in character. "O.K., now say, 'No amount of crying can bring him back.' "

Beady was still stretched out, listening. When her

character's name was mentioned, she stiffened again. I repeated my dialogue, and we finished with, "You are right, Letty, my darling. We'll forget all this. The captain will make you mine."

We embraced and then Beady scrambled to her feet. I took Pop's fedora back to his room. Even Katherine, who was Mom's pet, had to sneak in the back and return Mom's good fur and gloves. The magic spell was broken, but for a while each of us saw ocean waves, satin gowns, tuxedos, and poisoned goblets from the tar roof of the garage.

After my successful portrayal of Robert Montgomery, I was ready, Katherine thought, for my debut. Just how she thought she could inveigle me to get up before an audience on that rickety porch stage, I cannot say. I was not yet seven, and still almost pathologically shy. I hid under my mother's apron and clung to her legs if strangers looked at me. But Katherine costumed me in a yellow crepe-paper dress adorned with robin-egg blue ruffles and my Sunday sandals. I stood still while she sewed the ruffles on and fluted them with her fingers. She pinned an old brown shawl of Mom's around me so that the audience would have the thrill of seeing my costume only when the curtains parted. Then down the hill we marched to Alice Stewart's house.

Alice was a very pretty mulatto girl, my friend Bonnie's cousin and my first producer. She lived in the house near the creek next to the Polaskis; in fact, their clothesline spanned the path between the two houses. Alice loved to sing. She was outgoing and spirited and it was her idea to put on a show. She assembled the talent, dressed the stage, placed the fruit crates and benches out in the backyard. (There were lots of crates because Alice's father ran the dump.) A ticket booth was erected, where we sold yard-seat tickets for 3¢ each. If you crossed the creek and sat on a rock or a log on the hill, it only cost a penny. A lot of younger boys crashed the event; they climbed the trees over the creek and had gallery seats. A bench was reserved for Mrs. Polaski, who was still nursing. Everybody in Job's Hole came to that show, even the men who loafed on the bench at the store.

Alice had her brother string two army blankets up on a clothesline across the front porch. The performers could then rush into place privately, stand for a second to swallow their hearts and center their beings before the moment of exposure. When the curtains parted to reveal a blur of moon-faces, the performer would burst into song or dance or recitation.

Waiting in Alice's kitchen for our turns to come, we chirped like nervous crickets. I stood next to Katherine, who loyally sat by my side as she whispered last-minute instructions and kept fluting out the ruffles on my costume. "Now don't forget to curtsy when you start . . . take your time and speak up and say:

> '*Of all the colors I've ever seen,*
> *Red is the baddest one.*
> *I mean to have it grow right on top of your head.*'

Now here you put both hands on your head, O.K.?

> '*So lots of people call you "Red."* '

Pause.

> '*I know a man who loves to tease. . . .*
> *His head's as bald as my bare knees.*'

Just bend over and with both hands brush your knees. Then stand up and say:

'I'll tell him so, and then I'll run;'

Now go toward the exit. Stop. Face front and say:

'Red hair's better than having none!'

Curtsy and exit. O.K.?"

I listened intently to my sister, but I was petrified. Once the show started and I watched actors go on and then exit, bending over and laughing hysterically when it was over, exultant, excited, and relieved at having chanced danger, I grew anxious and bold in spirit. I could hardly wait for my turn. I even ventured away from Katherine's side and watched enraptured as Alice Stewart sang:

> *"It's only a shanty*
> *In old shanty town ..."*

The audience loved her. Her motions were so vivid and effective. She exited, exaggerating terror, deliberately buckling her knees and giggling. "Go on back," the other performers urged. "Encore!" And she went back, shaking her head and smiling. She put up her long-fingered, bejeweled hands and said, "O.K., O.K." Then she sang again:

> *"I'd give up a palace*
> *If I were a king.*
> *It's more than a palace,*
> *It's my everything ..."*

The audience joined her with:

> *"There's a queen waiting there,*
> *With silvery hair.*
> *In a shanty*
> *In old shanty town."*

She was glorious. When she finished, she was so comfortable, she moved scenery right in front of the audience.
She announced other acts with long, detailed introductions.
She laughed and cut up, and had the audience really going.
We couldn't get her off. By the time she got around to me, I
was like a racehorse raring to go. My sister jumped up from
her chair and said, "Now wait, honey, till they draw the
curtain for you. Alice, see that they draw the curtain for
Anna."

Alice went out and carefully drew the blankets. Then
she stepped in front and introduced me: "Ladies and Gen-
tlemen! Anna Jane Jackson!"

I wobbled to the center of the porch stage; the blanket
parted. The audience greeted me with applause. I curtsied
and put up my hands, imitating Alice's gesture to quiet
them. They laughed in recognition. Then I opened my
mouth and went into my recitation. My voice raced out
over the heads of the audience . . . over the creek . . . up the
hill to the gallery seats in the sky. I just acted my heart out.
Their laughter sent ecstatic thrills from my toes to the roots
of my hair. When I exited, there was a crash of applause
like the sea in one's ears when a wave breaks, and my knees
shook even more.

Alice Stewart tried to push me back out, but I didn't
have an encore. When she kept shoving me, I balked. I ran
away, out the back door, around the side of the house, up

the hill, and into my cellar. My heart was racing; my face was as hot as a burning light bulb. I sat near the root beer barrel, the pulsation of laughter in my throat; the rhythm of the poem raced through my mind.

I took an empty cardboard box and placed it on the crest of the hill in front of our house. I could still see part of the audience down in the valley across the creek. With a triumphant screech, I pushed myself off and went plummeting down the dirt hill. A ruffle from my crepe paper costume detached itself and caught in the breeze . . . a blue streamer dizzily whirling skyward.

Later, when my mother heard about my triumph, she was both pleased and surprised. "Well, wouldn't that take the cake," she said. "That little dickens won't open her mouth when we visit my relatives, but she'll get up before strangers!"

That night when Daddy came home, he had heard about my debut from the men in the store. "Well, well," he said when he saw me. "We have Sarah Bernhardt in family." Beady was so jealous she recited the thirty-two stanzas of "The Wreck of the Hesperus" for all of us after supper . . . nobody even knew she knew it.

As the weather grew better, Beady and I wandered farther from home in search of adventure. We heard cows mooing in a distant pasture and we realized that there was more going on around us than we had dreamed of. As we ventured out, Mom's fears increased. Mr. Kompesek, the farmer who owned those cows, shot at kids stealing pumpkins; one Hallowe'en, our neighbor Herby Orgruss lost an eye up there. Bonnie Stewart led us up that hill to wider, greener pastures, where her brother Clarence ran wild with Billy Klaus, the terror of Job's Hole.

Mom called him "poor white trash." His family lived in the house next to the Stewarts. Mr. Klaus was a foreign-born, handsome-looking Pole, who was as dark as his wife was fair. He tried to shoot her one Saturday night because he "caught her with a man."

She took her high heels off after that, cut her long stringy blonde hair, and went at her housework furiously. The suds flew from her washtub from then on, but Mom still didn't like her. When Daddy defended her, Mom practically had a tantrum. I knew Pop was "in" with the Klauses . . . I was with him when he brought Mrs. Klaus a bouquet of his flowers on a Sunday morning before the shooting. Pop was friendly and liked to put his arms around people; Mr. Klaus didn't like it. The talk was that Mr. Klaus was insanely jealous because Alice was so much younger than he. She had a young-girl figure, which she showed off to advantage. She encased her waist in a patent leather belt. She wore floral silk prints, which were "too tight for decency," Mom said and added, "She has that hooked nose and pinched face. Why she's as ugly as a mud fence. You wonder what men see in her." She also said, "I don't think it's any accident that all those children are fair like her. Why, you'd think just by the law of averages, one of them Klauses would have his dark hair or eyes."

Beady hints that Mom thought she was sweet on Pop because she took walks alone past our house a lot, and would giggle and flirt with Daddy at the pansy bed. I can't imagine how she managed to teeter about in those high heels on the cinder path, but she did. She also lingered to talk and laugh with the men who loafed on the bench down at the country store.

Her son, Billy, looked just like her. He had catty amber eyes and that same pointy nose and chin. The straight ends of his flaxen hair stuck out from his cap. I have cause to remember Billy.

One warm, sunny morning, Bonnie took Beady and me up the hill violet-picking and jarring grasshoppers. The grass was wet with dew. Billy Klaus, in overalls without a shirt, was playing up there with Clarence Stewart and Herby Orgruss. They were all about ten years old, while Beady was nine and Bonnie and I were seven. They started throwing pebbles at us and hiding and laughing behind trees. One nasty thing led to another and finally Billy Klaus, who wore his cap to the side à la Wallace Beery, said, "How about a hump?"

I didn't know what he meant but Bonnie spat at him and called him a filthy-mouthed pig. "I'm telling on you, brother," she said to Clarence. "See if I don't." Beady threw her violets in a shower at Billy and yelled, "Go home, stinker! Girls, run for your lives!"

My sandal had a buckle off, so as I started running I lost my shoe, slipped on the wet grass and fell. Billy, the huge oaf, pinned me to the ground and even though I kicked and squirmed, holding onto my underpants for dear life, I couldn't get away from him. I was hoarse from screaming. Beady and Bonnie stopped in the pasture, picked up my cry for help, shouting "Murder! Help!" at the top of their lungs. The cows stopped chawing grass, threw a lazy look my way, and lumbered further off, their udders swaying.

Mr. Kompesek, the farmer, once alerted, came running with his pitchfork in hand, and started for the hill. "What's happening in my field?" he shouted as he approached. Billy jumped to his feet and kicked me in the side before he ran off. Mr. Kompesek pulled me to my feet. His teeth were tobacco-stained. He stank of manure, nicotine, and underarm sweat. His knobby head was shaved up over his ears. I was convulsed with sobs. "All right," he said. "You frightened my cows wid your hollering. What the hell you say to that fellow? I don't want you coming around here doing those things on my land. Nice girls don't do bad things like you know about."

When I told my mother what had happened and what Mr. Kompesek said, she sputtered like a teakettle. "I don't want you playing with that Bonnie Stewart ever again. I don't trust any of those people. Don't you ever go into that pasture again. That vile Mr. Kompesek ought to be ashamed of himself. When your father comes home . . . Why, God only knows what could happen if you girls roam those lonely hills."

Mom was prophetic. That same summer Beady and I went back to the pasture and even wandered beyond it. We passed under barbed-wire fences and climbed over stone barricades to get to a tree with a wonderful Tarzan branch Bonnie told us about. We took turns swinging on it high over the creek. It was a hazardous and marvelous adventure. We were up there swinging at a dizzy height when a man passed. He was wearing a white shirt open at the throat and had a yellow straw fedora on his head. He was going about his business, and he looked respectable, so I said, "Hello."

He returned my greeting, and gradually realized that we were two little girls alone and offered to take me for candy. I was all set to go, but Beady was suspicious and said, "No, you don't. Mom doesn't know, so you can't." Then while I was swinging in the tree, he took Beady's hand and asked her to feel his thing. Beady kicked him and pulled away and said, "Let go of me! I'm telling my mother.

Run for your life, Runt." The alarm in her voice alerted me. I leapt from the swing and tore after her.

I could really run. When we got a safe distance from him, we stood and looked back. He was wagging his thing and waving a white hanky. Beady grew brave with distance and yelled, "Dirty rat! We don't want to see your ugly old thing. We're calling the police on you."

I was shocked and upset by his deception. I thought I was getting candy, but the man turned out to be vile and nasty. Though Beady and I promised each other not to tell Mom, Beady's need to brag got the best of her when we got home, and she blurted out that she had saved the Runt's life again. She described the man's candy bribe and his exposing his privates. On hearing this story, Mom went pale before she hit the ceiling.

Our two years in Job's Hole came to an abrupt end soon thereafter. Dishes flew into crates. Daddy could not stand up to Mom's determination to leave. But he had had enough as well; in fact, the Depression took its toll on the Scientific Beauty Shop, too. Miners and mill hands and even the Tarentum merchants were putting bowls on their heads and cutting their own hair. The die was cast. Daddy would precede us to New York and in a month's time, we'd move.

PART TWO

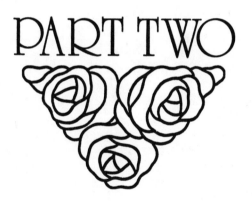

I f the moves in Pennsylvania were jarring, the big one to New York was cataclysmic. Uprooted from his land and flowers, Daddy set off to seek pie in the sky. It was 1933, the Depression held the whole country in its grips, and New York was where the jobs were. Daddy sold his barber shop in Tarentum and preceded us to New York to find a home and a new job.

The last evening in Job's Hole, we girls sat on Mom's hope chest, rolling our stockings and anklets, while she sorted our winter things. "Mind," she warned, "that you put the ones to be darned in that separate pile. There's nothing worse than holes in your socks for people to see. We don't want to be wearing shabby things in New York." Although it meant moving still farther away from her family, she seemed excited about the promise of New York, too. Leaving Job's Hole delighted her, and her happiness was infectious.

She tossed my brown hand-me-down coat from Aunt Gert onto the floor, announcing, "We'll get rid of this old thing." She had cut it down for me because it didn't fit her or anybody else, but to alter a large woman's coat to a child's size eight would have challenged the nimblest fingers. My arms got tangled in the sleeve linings. The black fur collar kept dangling loose because we never had the proper needles to attach it. "Anna is going to be the first to get a winter coat when we get to the new place," Mom explained.

I was thrilled beyond words; I had never owned a brand-new winter coat before, and, luxury of luxuries, *I* would finally be the donor of a hand-me-down. I swaggered about the room sucking up to Mom after this announcement. Beady of course was jealous and immediately started complaining about sharing a suitcase with me, but Mom placated her by saying, "Now, Beady, your good winter things are being packed in the hope chest with my good quilt, where they won't get all wrinkled and moth-eaten." But I was the one who'd get to sashay up and down Broadway in an elegant new winter coat.

Anticipating the move to New York put us all in a fever of excitement. Katherine tantalized me with her description of Manhattan's skyscrapers and ocean liners — images she'd gleaned from her movie-going — which had me believing that we'd be in with the swells and lead fast, gay lives now. I pictured us riding around in big cars and living in a penthouse overlooking the Statue of Liberty. Although I couldn't quite visualize Mom sitting cross-legged, crooking her little finger, and swigging gin, I dreamed of all of us being around "Manhattan Babies," up 'til three, and tap-dancing on Forty-second Street.

My dreams of city life were clearly fanciful, but nothing could have prepared us for the Old Mill Landing in Brooklyn, where Pop chose to settle. A contemporary account from the Brooklyn *Eagle* described the area in pleasantly neutral terms: "The individual with disdain for the comforts of civilization and an eye for the picturesque can still get himself a house overlooking the melancholy reaches of Jamaica Bay for approximately $7.00 a month. The Old Mill Landing is not more than a mile away from the push-carts, cinemas, and polylingual restaurants of Brownsville. From Crescent Street station on the elevated line a bus runs every 15 minutes." The Old Mill Landing was a minor resort abounding in swamps. A network of grey weathered boardwalks forked out from an old gristmill that gave the area its name and led to damp summer cottages sitting up on wharf beams in the middle of Jamaica Bay. Pop saw them in summer at high tide with a moon dancing on the water, and rented one for us.

We arrived at low tide, when the water had sunk back from the black mud, leaving a soggy marsh littered with orange peels and hideous green scum and stinking of decomposed vegetation. Mom hated it on sight. Having just come from Job's Hole, one of Pop's worst blunders as far as she was concerned, she was sent into a fit by this new debacle. "My God in heaven," she moaned, "he's gone and outdone himself with this rat hole." But I had inherited my father's eye for the picturesque and was delighted at living in a cottage by the sea. The idea of running along the railed wooden walks and seeing sea birds skim skyward over the tides into the September sunsets enraptured me. I grew pensive and romantic, dreaming of Dick Powell paddling me up a lagoon as I trailed my hand through the cool water. The Old Mill's thousands of mosquitoes and gnats were excluded from my fantasy, but I fancied fireflies flickering in the distance as my lover wooed me on Jamaica Bay.

Mom wasn't going to settle into this cottage without a

struggle, though. Fleeing back to Ma'am in Pittsburgh was unthinkable now, so she set her sights on escaping the Old Mill and finding us a respectable place to live herself once summer passed.

One morning shortly after we arrived, Mom sent me to buy a loaf of bread, fig newtons, and eight bananas for a dime. "Pick firm ones which are still a little green," she instructed, "and watch them weigh the pound of fig newtons." She gave me a dollar and added, "You can have two cents for candy." The tide was high, the sun was warm. I went dancing barefoot toward the store when suddenly the wind stole my dollar right out of my hand and tossed it recklessly into the tide. I watched in impotent horror as it floated off into the tall marsh grasses, out of reach and sight. I was several boardwalks away from home when I set up a cry for Mamma, which brought a woman in a kimono and her half-clad husband to their window, peeking through curtains of weathered chintz.

"What wuz ya goin' up the store for?" the woman asked. "Jeeze, maybe you could ask Ernie to charge it." I ran off crying for Mamma, who hobbled back to the spot with me, broom in hand, to see if there was some way to retrieve the dollar. But it was all in vain.

"You should've kept that dollar folded in your hand or in your shoe. Couldn't you see how windy it is here? And all those open rails. I thought of giving you a fifty-cent piece, but I was afraid you'd lose it in a crack in the board-walk. Oh my God, with times as they are and you go and lose all that money. I'll just have to tell your father. He'll wonder what I did with my allowance."

She droned on, rubbing it in until I began to tremble

with indignation. Covering my ears, I screamed, "Why do you blame me for what the wind did?"

Not too long after the lost-dollar incident, Lil, our strange-looking neighbor in the kimono, came knocking on our door. Her hair was cut like Buster Brown's and she spoke with such a thick Brooklyn accent we thought she came from some exotic place. "Hell no," she said, contradicting my mother. "What, are ya, kiddin'? I was born right heah in good ol' Brooklyn, up to Crescent Street."

She stood in our walkway at the open door. Mom was ashamed to invite her in because the "rat hole" was dank and "furnished in awful taste." Lil stood outside of everyone's doorway, though, and even when invited in, she sedately refused. "No, I won't step in; I'm not dressed," she said, indicating her bathrobe and bedroom slippers.

"There's gonna be a hurricane tonight, missus. When the mister comes home, you betta warn him and the kids. I gotta feelin' it'll be a whopper. Last one floated people's houses right away. We all hadda 'vacuate and lie on our stomachs. Betta take your prayer books if you got 'em, 'cause you'll need His help with Her." ("Her" this time was not the dollar, but the hurricane.)

Though we didn't evacuate, I remember that storm vividly. The rain cascaded on the roof. Daddy ran in from work soaked and breathless, eyeglasses in hand, his skin showing pink through his white shirt and trousers. The rain had plastered his hair to his head and the water sloshing in his shoes stained his white socks brown. I rushed to remove one shoe and Beady the other as leftover raindrops gathered on his chin before dropping off his face. He seemed gleeful and exhilarated by the storm.

The lights flickered out, the radios went dead, lightning cut the sky, and thunder boomed, shaking our house. The gale winds stripped a shutter half off, leaving it flapping this way and that in the wind. The back door flew open and right off its hinges. My mother, Katherine, and even Beady were rigid with fear. Only Daddy and I seemed to enjoy the storm. "Oh boy," he said, "that's some rain what we having. Reminds me of 'Wreck of the Hesperus,' eh Anna, so damned good thing we not on boat."

"We might as well be, John," Mom said angrily. "If we live through this awful night, I'm going to take the bus into City Line with you in the morning and find a decent place for us to live."

She spoke for my sisters as well, for they hated the Old Mill too. Only Dad shared my wistful feelings about that bygone place. I enjoyed running along the planks and seeing into people's private rooms in the cottages abutting the boardwalk. The flickering fireflies and the stars winking in the water at high tide, even the little bugs making pretty circles in the midnight blue waters, created a romantic yearning in me for the old days when the boardwalk was decked out with Japanese lanterns for the regatta races on the Bay and lovely ladies twirled their parasols and swished along in long flowing gowns. The Old Mill, itself now just a shell of a building, evoked the ghosts of long-gone happy crowds; it felt eerie and awesome watching the sky drop through the holes in the roof.

I was my father's daughter in that I shunned middle-class conventions of comfort and respectability. I thrilled to adventure and daring. To me, Dad's choices of places to live had style. I just didn't appreciate Mom's problems of coping with housework and failing physical strength. I would have liked spending the winter at the Old Mill, but Mom had no intention of staying in a freezing cottage with the pump shut off. She would have her way; the storm marked the end of our stay in the home on stilts by the sea.

Before Thanksgiving, we moved to our first "decent" apartment on Forbell Avenue, near Ozone Park in Queens. This move marked a step up the social ladder: we had six rooms, steam heat, and a hot water boiler in our own bathroom. During the Depression, twenty-five dollars a month was a lot of rent money for Pop to muster up. He worked long hours for a barber on Liberty Avenue trying to make ends meet. Though Mom complained that lights for six rooms gave Con Ed more of our allowance than seemed fit, and the hot water boiler used too much gas, she nonetheless bought a parlor suite set on time and Daddy purchased a secondhand rug for the living room. My penthouse dream was realized—we lived on the top floor over a store. But like most of our homes, it too would only be temporary.

City life seemed to uncover a whole new personality in me. I no longer hid behind my mother's skirts, but emerged from a quiet, timid child into a show-off and hellion. My mother called me a "rip" and "rapscallion," and said, "As true as God's in heaven, that child will come to a bad end. She'll end up in a house of ill repute if she doesn't mend her ways." But I continued to be bad and willful. It was while living on Forbell Avenue that I began my life of crime—thieving, gambling, and telling racy jokes. My chief tempter in these adventures was my friend Mary Donne. She told me all the details of the sex act as she knew them, and my mind was preoccupied with the unsavory and puzzling aspects of people "doing it" — until I learned to gamble.

Mary's older sister Winnie taught Beady to play cards, and Beady in turn taught me. We played obsessively. Our favorite games were gin and casino until Mary stole some dice from her father's bureau and all four of us developed a passion for shooting craps. Before long, our games became violent. "That was not your point!" someone would scream. We played in the hallway under the transom, and sometimes a die would fly out into the shadows. While retrieving it, the thrower would lie about what number was showing. "I win. That was my point."

"Kiss up to God, dirty liar — and no fins behind your back. Cheater! Louse! Sneak!"

We played for our jewelry and the clothes off our backs. When I won a gold chain pendant from Winnie, the roof fell in on our gambling racket. Her mother came up to our apartment on Sunday morning and Pop answered the door. Mrs. Donne held out a pudgy hand. "I want Winnie's ruby back, Mr. Jackson. That pendant was her confirmation gift from my sister Sally. I don't know about you, but I've warned my girls that if they play craps again, I'll crack their heads open."

Daddy summoned us. "Anna, Beatrice, come in here. What is all about?"

We both talked at once. "We won, Daddy. They have our good hanky and my blue beads. It was my point," I said with dignity. "I want my black velvet hair ribbon back, and my six curlers too," Beady added. Daddy shut us up with an order. "Go and give back everything you won in gambling."

We pulled out the boxes hidden under our beds and dug out the bead box for the necklaces, the anklets, and

Mary's Saint Christopher medal, and gave them all back in exchange for our own precious possessions.

Though that incident suspended our hallway trysts with the Donne girls, Mary and I continued our thrilling life of crime. One time we went on a spree in Woolworth's on Liberty Avenue, stealing indiscriminately: I took a bracelet with a Scotty dog on a chain, a green rubber eraser, a compass, some jelly jar rings, a pair of yellow baby booties, and a nest of metal Jell-O molds, and stuffed them all into my bloomers. I started down the aisle, wobbling and rattling as I went, my dress misshapen from my loot.

The manager, Mr. Fox, stood in my path at the exit doors and with nary a word turned me around by the scruff of my neck and led me through the store to the back office. Mary was nowhere to be seen. I could feel flames of humiliation scalding my cheeks as I slowly mounted the strange staircase to the office, through a swinging gate into the cubicle of dark wood paneling topped with frosted glass. I realized when we reached this secluded office that I would have to extract my loot from its hiding place. My heart beat like a jackhammer. Mr. Fox sat down and calmly began to wait, holding out his hand and looking at me knowingly.

"What's your name?"

"Anna Jane Jackson."

"Where do you live?"

"On Forbell Avenue."

"Are you the barber's kid?"

"Yes," I admitted and broke down crying.

"O.K., Anna Jane," he said, "are we going to call your father about this?" Mr. Fox was a customer of Daddy's. At the mention of Pop, I heaved sobs. "O.K.," Mr. Fox held out his hand steadily and said, "now let's have what you stole."

My knees began to quiver violently. I turned slightly away and picked up my cotton print dress, stuck my hand down the matching bloomers and pulled out the hateful loot piece by piece. Mr. Fox just watched me, shaking his head, nonplussed. "O.K., kid; what else?" Each dumb object brought looks of confusion and sighs of exasperated disgust from him. "All right, girlie. You better stay out of here. If I ever catch you again, I'll call your old man first thing."

He stood up, held open the swinging gate and shoved me through it. I was dismissed. I preceded him as we walked down the main aisle to the exit. He pulled out a set of keys on a long chain and began swinging them around his index finger as we threaded our way past sales clerks and customers. It was the longest walk I had ever taken.

I raced home, trying not to cry, and as I ran, a rubber jelly ring bounced around in my bloomers, a sickening reminder of my crime. I was panicked that the ring would work its way out through the elasticized leg. I reached our entrance, and skidded to a full stop at the cellar door. I fished frantically in my pants for this last shred of evidence, yanked open the door, and threw the ring into the musty darkness. It hit the face of an ascending figure. I could not see who it was, but the voice riveted me to the spot. "God my, daughts, what the hell you trying to do to me? You scared wits out of your father."

But it wasn't Mr. Fox or the close call with my father that finally cured me of stealing. It was an issue of fifteen dollars and my own sense of self-hatred that worked the trick.

I found the money on the street one day and, delighted

with my booty, I ran home and gave it to my mother. She made me swear not to tell my father about it. The next day she went off to Queen's County Hospital for a week's cure for her bad leg, leaving Katherine in charge of the family finances. The fifteen dollars were kept under the rug in the living room and the change went into a jar in the cupboard. When I saw Mary Donne that day, I just had to brag about finding so much money. She was very impressed, and when I showed her the exact spot where I came upon this incredible fortune, she asked, "What's your share?"

"Well, my mother's gonna buy me something really special," I said.

"Why don't you just steal some and we'll go to the movies?"

And steal it I did. For three days in a row I took a dollar. Mary Donne and I bought frappes at the ice-cream parlor (frappes were two scoops of ice cream in a *tall glass* — with hot fudge on and a cherry on top — different from a sundae, served in a lowly dish); we rode the elevated train and ran through the cars, laughing and showing off and acting silly until it was time to go to the movies. On the third day of our spree I came home late, sick to my stomach, and went to bed. When my father came home from work, Katherine tearfully told him about the missing money. Somehow Katherine reported it without involving my mother and disclosing her hiding place under the rug. I listened in the dark bedroom and heard with growing dread my sister itemize all she had spent down to the very last penny. Three dollars remained unaccounted for. When I didn't eat supper for the third consecutive night, I became a prime suspect. I was careless and gave myself away; my pockets bulged with candy wrappers, and chocolate stained the corners of my mouth. When Beady tattled that she had seen me coming out of the Earl Theater with "that other awful brat," the jig was up. Trying a last resort for mercy and pity, I took to my bed, groaning, and began writhing in pain from stomach gas. This was the beginning of my first colitis attack, a malady that would plague me throughout childhood.

My father appeared at the foot of my bed and pulled the light cord.

"Anna," he said, "what is meaning of this?"

I burst into tears. "I only took what was my share," I blurted out. "I found fifteen dollars," and choking and gurgling I tried to weasel out by incriminating my mother. "Mamma promised me she'd buy me something special, but she didn't. She told me not to tell you."

My father took the news of the deception and switched out the light. "I'll take care of this matter when the mother returns," he said quietly.

Katherine was sent in to give me milk of magnesia. She was quiet and subdued, ashamed to face me. Even Beady, who normally enjoyed rubbing it in when I got in trouble, sensed my self-hatred and was quiet. Somehow I knew I'd have to deal with my conscience, and it was an experience I'll never forget. It wasn't so much the stealing that troubled my soul, it was my incriminating my mother and breaking my promise to her. I felt like a worm.

I wrestled with this moral dilemma on my own, remembering things my mother and father had taught me.

My mother's lessons in morality presented no problems or questions because they were absolutes. Had she found out about my stealing, she would have blamed it on bad company and would have forbidden me to ever play with Mary again, rattling off one of her proverbs, "Show me your company and I'll tell you who you are."

But my father taught us morality by using allegories. They came on impulse, like bolts of lightning. They were always erratic and always confusing.

"You see, certain things are best learned in this life to clear out the jungle of the minds before you have chance to make mistakes. Father has obligation to guide the children in ways of morality. Without the morals the mankind is in jungle. Sometimes we have to illustrate for children. We have to clear path, so to speak. Sometimes father or mother must endure great pain in order for children to develop proper outlook in life.

"Over there in old country a farmer and his son worked on land together. They were poor peasants. As they were hoeing one summer day, a soldier comes through their gate, holding his hand on breast. Father watches from a distance, does not hear what stranger is saying to his son. He surmises that soldier is in trouble because he sees blood on the hand and from little distance away he hears tinkle of few coins being offered. All money what he has, so boy will hide him. Father realizes that wounded soldier is running away from army. He sees son pocket money and together they are crossing rapidly to barn. After hiding the soldier, the boy comes back out to wheelbarrow and resumes work. Father says nothing. He figures, 'No — let him handle; let him do.'

"Little while later, while still working in field, there comes more soldiers, officers, three or four, very rapidly coming toward boy. Boy looks up and wonders, 'What the devil is this? What's coming there?' The soldiers come in and they start heated conversation with the boy. Father can tell from gestures they are excited.

" 'Did you see by any chance soldier come this way?' "

"No, boy shakes his head; no, he didn't see that.

" 'Uh, huh,' Sergeant looks and sees in boy's face maybe something suspicious. Father is in the meantime coming a little closer, but wants to see on the sidelines what's going to happen. All right!

"So the sergeant says to the boy, 'We think maybe he came this way; you sure you saw nobody?'

" 'Oh, no I didn't see. No, I'm sorry.'

"So soldiers look around, nodding heads, you know, and looking at each other. They say nothing, but maybe, you know, they look on the ground. Could be little spot blood, something. Could be from kill chicken. All right. So they are about to leave and then sergeant gets idea. He goes into pocket. He pulls out gold watch on chain and dangles it for boy to see. He says, 'You're sure you saw nobody? No soldier come this way?'

"Father looks and sees his son point to barn. Father can't believe his eyes. And soldier drops the watch in boy's hand. They go over there and pull fellow out the barn and roughneck him a little. As captive passes by the boy he tries to meet his eye, but boy lowers head. Captors push soldier out gate and they are gone. Now father doesn't know what to think, what to do. He is, so to speak, resigned. He goes and gets shotgun from the barn. He calls to his son to come behind barn and he shoots him.

"The father could not have traitor for son."

"My God, John," my mother said. "Why would you be telling the girls a story like that? They won't be going into the army."

"They must learn, in this life, they must learn what traitor is. Man could live with anything, but he cannot live with traitor in children, in friend, in other mankind."

I'd been a traitor, but no one would shoot me behind the barn. My ten-year-old heart had learned the price of treachery when I squealed on my mother, and didn't want to pay it again.

On the day we moved from Forbell Avenue, I remember standing in the empty living room and watching the movers roll up the wine-colored carpet. I wished it had all been a bad dream and that the three dollars would suddenly reappear. Instead, there was just dust and lint and the head of a paper doll on the scarred wooden floor.

The wine-colored rug had to be folded under to fit the front room of our new apartment at 1125 Liberty Avenue in City Line, a three-flight walk-up in a four-family tenement. Tucked between the A&P and the Army and Navy Store, our entrance was flanked on one side by stands holding men's socks, boots, shirts, and goggles, and on the other side by the A&P's milk-bottle crates and empty cardboard boxes. The row of four mailboxes, equipped with speakers and bells over which a faded sign read "Out of order," showed one blank insert where our name would go, next to the MacIntyres, Ingineros, and Halstons. We would live on the top floor, left, sharing the hall toilet with the MacIntyres. A long dark hallway stretched beyond the vestibule to wooden steps lit by a weak electric bulb. My excitement at moving dimmed as I looked back at the sunlight's futile attempt to cut past the El posts and spread itself in the doorway. I would climb these stairs for eight years, until I was eighteen, and always be struck by that extreme transition from sunlight to blackness, which caused temporary blindness. This was the place where I'd grow to young womanhood.

I didn't really feel homesick for Pennsylvania until we

moved to that tenement on Liberty Avenue. Then the enormity of our move to Brooklyn struck me, challenging me with vast adjustments to make: a new school, new people, new sounds, new games. Instead of the hills and fields, the creek and the spring, our new backyard was a stingy fenced-in rectangle where the A&P stored empty cartons. Though Daddy tried his best to plant a garden, his effort was in vain. There just wasn't enough soil or sun. There was nowhere for me to jar grasshoppers and catch butterflies, no rocks in the woods to overturn after a rain in search of worms. I missed the light tickle of a ladybug's legs and the crawl of furry caterpillars up my arms.

In Pennsylvania, Beady and I had taken great pride in our country knowledge. There was no insect or variety of worm we couldn't identify. We knew their fears, their excretions, their hiding habits. Sitting on our haunches until our legs grew numb with needles, we'd watch worms bore holes in the black earth. If we picked them up, the pretty green and yellow ones would curl themselves up in our palms and play dead. The grasshoppers were our favorites. They were nearly impossible to catch and keep. They fought for freedom even in a closed hand. In our curiosity and superior strength we could be cruel. We delegged the grasshoppers and dissected the worms. We had no conscience, no awareness that they would one day have their go at us.

In Brooklyn I was repelled by bedbugs and roaches and mice cruelly strangled in mousetraps. City pavement called for shoes at all times. And, worst of all, Brooklyn brought estrangement from my sisters.

Beady was thirteen and began to grow odd and self-conscious as she matured. We still competed with each other verbally, but our interests changed. She lived in hair curlers, wore loose blouses and hunched her shoulders to hide her new breasts. She puffed powder over skin blotches, whispered to Mom, and hid herself while dressing.

Not only did I feel the loss of Beady, but Kay suddenly leaped into her senior high school year. No more acting out of movies or reading on the hill. I missed eating sour grass and collecting Daddy's bitter dandelion leaves. When I saw a lone buttercup in the empty lot on my way to school, or a yellow wet-the-bed shooting up between the cracks on one of the quiet tree-lined streets where I played, I'd go crazy with longing. I missed slurping cold water from the mountain spring. When I put my mouth under our green-stained kitchen spigot, the thin, warm stream tasted coppery.

The serenity of the outhouse was replaced by a hall toilet in constant demand. It stank of the disinfectant C.N. The porcelain tub in the kitchen was, I guess, more convenient and up-to-date than the round grey galvanized tub we lugged from the cellar to our kitchen in Job's Hole, but even Mom admitted that the sweet smell of heated rainwater was better than the endless waiting for the rusty piped water of our tenement. She preferred, however, pulling in her wash from the back kitchen window to carting her basket heavy with linens up a hill to a country clothesline.

In the summer, when the bedroom doors had to be left open, you could see clear through from the kitchen to the parlor windows. The racket and the vibrations created by the El trains hammering past interrupted many a conversation and frayed all our nerves. Those moving trains had an unsettling effect: a blur of color and a distortion of faces. Passengers' eyes looking in gave me the eerie feeling of living in a fishbowl. Sometimes, in retaliation, I pressed my tongue and flattened my nose on the window pane and crossed my eyes for all the train passengers to see as it raced by.

Another irritating aspect of living on Liberty Avenue in the shadow of that El rail was our having to lean out the parlor window at a perilous angle to see the marquee of the City Line Cinema across the street. Even then, only the title of the second feature was visible.

When someone took a bath, it caused a major annoyance because everyone else had to stay out of the kitchen. Katherine was constantly secluding herself in the tub prior to her numerous dates. Even though Mom had trouble climbing up to the tub, she too claimed her time for long and thorough spongings. But no matter who washed, I had to reuse the tepid water, and there was no playing there — it was business — just plain "get into that tub before the water gets too cold." There was just so much hot water in the tank, and the gas was too dear for me to be wasting it.

These constant struggles for privacy, aggravated by the new estrangement from my sisters, led me to seek a life in the streets. I turned my interest to Lincoln Avenue. From our kitchen window I could see into the backyards of my would-be friends who lived there. I could hear from my fire escape the street's sounds, the screeches of boys playing stoop-ball and the shrill calls of girls to one another, "Angie, where's Lucy? Can she come down the street to play?"

Those enticing street sounds brought me around the block one Saturday afternoon that spring to seek playmates. What a delight to see a girl about my age with long red curls and a big yellow pinwheel bow clipped to her head, standing on a stoop near a light pole. I eyed her and cautiously edged closer, bouncing my ball and chanting:

"Hello, Bill.
Where you going, Bill?
Up town, Bill.
What for, Bill?
To pay the gas bill ..."

I flung my leg over the ball, misjudged, missed, and had to chase it into the gutter.

"You missed," hissed the girl with the pinwheel bow, smiling coyly.

"I know I did — I always miss on the last line," I confessed.

"Hey kid, what's your name? ..."

"Anna Jane. ..."

"Anna Jane what? ..."

"Anna Jane Jackson."

"Where was you born?"

"Pennsylvania."

"What's your father?"

"A barber."

"No, I mean, what's his nationality?"

"He's a foreigner. ..."

"Where do you go to school?"

"P.S. Two Fourteen."

"Who you votin' for, Roosevelt or Landon?"

"Roosevelt."

"He's a Jew."

"Well, maybe Norman Thomas."

"Who's he?"

"I don't know."

She came down to the first step and threw a leg over the black iron railing. I took my turn — "What's your name?"

"Jean Margaret Murphy."

"Where are you from?"

"Canarsie."

"Where's that?"

"You take the El— to the last stop. But we moved here last May—My Uncle Joe is the super of—" she pointed to the four-family dwelling "—this whole building —and my father works in the Navy Yard." She continued in a singsong voice, "And I'm a Catholic and I go to Saint Sylvester's—and I'm gonna be making my first holy communion in May. I'm going for my dress Sat'day—I'm scared stiff. I shoulda made it last year 'cause I came of age but I had scarlet fever."

"Why are you scared?" I asked.

"Because I'll have to go to confession and all that."

"My cousin Cecelia made her communion, she said you're not allowed to touch the wafer with your teeth."

"You Catholic?" Jean Margaret asked incredulously. Daddy's being a foreigner had thrown her off.

"Yes. On my mother's side . . . all my cousins made their communion and confirmation," I volunteered. "My father was Catholic too, but he quit."

Jean Margaret did a comic double take. She dropped her mouth open in fake surprise, grabbed her head in her two palms and said, "Oh no! Is that how come you have to go to public school?"

"My father thinks it's better," I answered.

Jean Margaret wrinkled her nose and then stuck her tongue out on one side of her mouth—her new second teeth had green tartar on them—"Not better than Saint Sylvester's," she said. "Only bad thing about our school is we have to wear those dark wool uniforms and they itch and the collars are stiff like anything. The nuns are nice, though, except if you get Sister Sam. Guess what? My brother Frankie had her and she wouldn't let him in her class 'til he cut his nails — he had to have a manicure and a clean handkerchief every single day. Sister Alice Marie hits with a ruler if you talk; or, God forbid, you don't know your catechism. You can't be late — ever — guess what? I was never absent, never late all last term."

Suddenly she got a strange look on her face. She motioned to me with her finger to come closer and whispered, "Do you have a boyfriend?"

"No," I answered, blushing.

Jean Margaret sat on the first step, pulled her dress taut over her knees, and then punched it down between her legs. "I have," she confided. "You wanna know who I love of all the boys in my class? Swear to God, hope to die, you won't tell anybody in the whole world? Kiss up to God," she said and demonstrated by kissing her pinky.

I kissed up to God, though I wouldn't even know who she loved and I really didn't care.

"Gene Benevello," she said. "He's from around the corner where you live. He kissed me," she squealed, her face flushed. She stuck her tongue out and popped her eyes again. Then springing up, she asked in her normal voice, "Do you want to play Flip Cards?"

"I don't know how."

"I'll show you," she said and ran into her hallway where she fished around behind the double doors. I could see her shadow from behind the frosted glass. Then she reappeared with some little round Dixie Cup cards, which had waxy pictures of movies stars on them. "See these?" she asked very seriously. "Now here's what, you flip a card and if a picture side comes up, you win — O. K.?"

"Are you gonna marry him?"

"Marry Gene?" she whispered, blushing. "I am never, never, never getting married. Don't you know anything? Do you know what the man does to you when you get married, stupid?"

"What?" I asked, though I knew perfectly well; hadn't I fought off a rapist when I was only seven and had seen that other man's ugly old thing? I knew when you were married and going to have a baby that your belly got swollen and I knew you had to give your titty to the baby. I told Jean Margaret all I knew. She listened squinty-eyed and was very impressed and enlightened by my experiences.

"You know what?" she said, settling herself on the stoop and punching her dress down between her legs again, "You could have a baby if you sit on the terlit after a man makes pee pee. That's why when my brother Frankie even makes, I won't sit on my own terlit. My mother says 'Never, never sit on any terlit,' unless you have to make the other — then you can, but not for pee pee."

"Well, I know that too," I said. "Is it hard to learn the catechism?" I asked, changing the subject.

"Oh sure. You gotta know the whole book and answer all the questions the priest or the sister asks you. God sees and hears everything so you can never, never, never lie."

"I know," I said.

Every day thereafter, I went around the corner to play. Jean Margaret and I flipped the Dixie Cup cards, but mostly we talked of boys and God and sometimes about Roosevelt. Jean Margaret did a lot of bragging about how smart she was. "Guess what?" she'd say. "I got a hundred in arithmetic, ninety-eight in English composition, ninety-eight on my history test; I have more gold stars than anybody else in my class so I'm probably going to get the prize.

I have the highest average in my whole room so I always get to be monitor — I always have to help Sister. Even Sister Superior likes me the best, so I have to go on errands for her." She always made it sound as though her brilliance and popularity were crosses she had to bear. She said a lot of dumb things, but I was fascinated by her knowledge of religion.

She knew about the Eucharist and how it was a sign. "It looks like bread — well it looks more like a candy Necco Wafer, see, but it is really the flesh of Christ. The wine is His blood. God said, 'He who eats my flesh and drinks my blood abides in me and in Him.' " She'd tell me all this in her singsong voice, hopping up and down and whirling around as she spoke. She loved making herself dizzy. "When I make communion, I'll have to fast for twenty-four hours, starting right after supper.

"My Aunt Lil and my grandmother are coming for my holy communion. So is my cousin Eleanor. Guess what? She's a Rockette and she dances at Radio City Music Hall." Then Jean Margaret continued her litany, but this time her monologue dealt with the Rockettes. "Guess what? My cousin Eleanor went to Paris and did the military march. Guess what? She gets paid forty-eight fifty a week and you have to be five foot four and you have to be eighteen. She had to go to Valetta's to learn to tap, toe, and acrobat."

Jean Margaret's monologues would last until the streetlights came on and windows flew open and mothers, sisters, and brothers called out through the neighborhood: "Jean Margaret, come for supper!" "Tom-meeeee — Tom! Thomas Murphy — Pop wants you"; "Ginny — Vi-r-ginnia — home!"

Then I would wander off to my house, noticing the store lights on Liberty Avenue go on one by one. The overhead train windows blurred into a yellow glow and green sparks flew as the wheels gnashed the rails. Darkness penetrated our hallway; the landlord was our superintendent, so he saw that only the one dim light on the first-floor landing was ever turned on. The door to the vestibule was usually left ajar; anyone could enter and disappear into the shadows. I would race down the dark entrance hall in terror of some ghost or bad man lurking in a corner, pass the cellar door, run toward the first floor landing, and on up to our flat.

As June — and Jean Margaret's communion — approached, the days grew longer and the streetlights came on later. We spent these extra hours together, playing jacks and jumping rope. The boys put up a hoop on the lamppost and regularly darkened the street by hitting the light with their basketball. Then they would ask us to play hide-and-seek, whip-the-lash, or ring-a-levio, and we'd hide and kiss the boys in the cellarways. But we both gave up those games as communion drew near, mostly because when we played ring-a-levio the boys got fresh when they caught us.

As I heard more about God and nuns and priests, a swell of religious feeling made me long for the experience of holy communion too. I dreamed of looking like a bride, all in white with a garland on my head. The idea of a veil sent me into a transport of delight. I would carry a missal of white leather with gold-bound pages, and purple, red and yellow satin ribbons as markers to holy pictures of Christ and His bleeding heart, and Mary, Our Mother, the Blessed Virgin. Snow white became my favorite color. I'd have snow white shoes, snow white socks, and snow white underthings. I saw myself holding two doves and floating a foot off the ground. People would kneel as I humbly cured them by the fervor of my belief. Only the whites of my eyes could be seen by the common herd.

My wicked ways were on the mend. I stopped picking up butts from the gutter; there was no more smoking with the MacIntyre girls in the hall. I did not lie or talk dirty. I obeyed my mother and stopped gambling altogether. Kay and Beady called me "Saint Anne" in disgust.

As for my father, he seemed not to notice my new religious fervor until he caught me selling Father Coughlin's *Social Justice* at the Grant Avenue El stop on Liberty Avenue.

Jean Margaret and I took turns holding the can into which the proceeds went. We were on the corner from three-thirty to five-thirty each afternoon. One day, I was hopping on the steel steps of the Grant Avenue Station waiting as the train came in, when Katherine came bouncing down on her way home from John Adams High School.

"Why are you playing on these stairs?" she asked. "People don't want to be tripping over you, you know, Anna Jane."

"I'm working, see." I held up my can and showed her the newspapers.

"You better ask Daddy about that," she warned, before she sashayed off, throwing me a suspicious look.

Not heeding her advice, I joined Jean Margaret at the El station again the following day. Pop saw me from his barbershop window across the avenue. I was making a transaction with my newspapers and did not see him approach. When he came upon me, I was busy counting change for a customer.

"Hello, daughts," he said. "What you got there under the arm?"

I went on the defensive immediately; "Social Justice"

seemed like a magic phrase. I suspected that the mention of
Father Coughlin might make him angry, so I slurred his
name, and emphasized the "Social Justice."

"Yeah," Pop said. "Yeah, where did you get these?"
he inquired.

"My girl friend gets them, Daddy, and I'm helping
her."

"Uh huh, well . . . I think maybe you better give them
to her and I think we have little talk tonight when I finish
work — most important for your future enlightenment,
daughts. You give these to your friend and you go on home
to the mother and I gonna see you later and we gonna
discuss just what is all about."

"I have to go home, my mother wants me," I said to
Jean Margaret, giving her my unsold papers and my can of
coins. I didn't really dread my father's lecture — when he
was philosophical, he was very gentle and usually obscure. I
felt rather a sickening disappointment about my future
plans with the Church, though. I somehow knew my father
could complicate and confuse the issue.

Pop was cheerful when he came home. It was pay-day.
He had had his schnapps at Dutche's Bar, then stopped in
the delicatessen and bought rye bread with seeds and some
sauerkraut. He invited me to join him at the table. I had
eaten earlier, but I loved sucking the crust of the bread and
drinking the sauerkraut juice. Daddy nibbled the caraway
seeds with his front teeth like a squirrel. "That's most marvelous bread. They bake fresh today, you know. Man
doesn't need too much else — bread and wine, daughts,
bread is staff of life and wine unlocks the soul."

"It unlocks your tongue is what it does, Daddy," my
mother said.

"Nothing in the world wrong with that. Just depends what you talk about, wifey dear," Pop bantered. "You know that your Anna was selling the newspapers today up near my shop? She thought father would approve, I'm sure. Poor thing didn't realize that she is being used by the fascists. She didn't understand what means all this."

"What in heaven's name are you ranting about, John? What was it you were selling, Anna?" my mother asked.

"Father Coughlin's *Social Justice*," I answered.

"Your Irish priest — what's up in Detroit, Stella — that's who the Anna is working for. He's some cute fella. He likes making fancy speeches on radio about poor people, while he's lining his pockets with their hard-earned money. He's a friend of the Ford, you know who is Henry Ford, daughts?"

"Just because one priest is bad, and I'm not saying he is, mind you, is no reason for you to ridicule my people," Mom said.

Pop shook his head tolerantly and grinned. "Anna — " his voice got softer " — what I'm trying to illustrate for you is how this man is not true Christian. How easy it is to be trapped by nice-sounding words and the bribe of medals. Same thing whether over there Saint Sylvester gives you Bleeding Heart medal, or voodoo palm what you hang over your bed in room there." Mom practically stormed about the room in a fury at this.

I was caught up in the whirlwind of emotion and confusion. "I just want to make my communion. And I have to wear a white dress so I get absolution for my sins," I argued.

Daddy's jaw fell. He took off his glasses, rubbed his eyes, nodded, and then said, "Yuh, I understand. I don't know at ripe old age of ten which sins you think you committed, but I think maybe you like that wedding dress little girls wear with the veil and the flowers. That finery is very enticing, but not utilitarian." He retired to the parlor.

Mom, sensing my mood, said, "If we could afford it, Anna, I'd like to see at least one of my children confirmed; but with Katherine graduating, we just can't afford it. Maybe next year we'll be better off." She hugged me to her for a moment and then reached for her newspaper. "Bring me that other chair, honey, so I can elevate my bad leg. There's a good girl.

"You wonder, don't you," she asked absentmindedly as she thumbed through the pages of the *Daily News*, "what the world is coming to?"

I didn't want to get into a discussion with her about the state of the world, so I went into the bedroom I shared with my sisters. Beady was in the parlor with Daddy, doing her current events homework. I could hear my father discussing Haile Selassie and Mussolini with her. Katherine was out cheerleading at a basketball game and hadn't come home yet.

I crawled under the bed and stealthily pulled a box out. It was from A&S department store in Brooklyn. As I opened it, all white tissue bulged up. The white net dress was folded neatly and even the little puffed sleeves were stuffed with tissue; the waist was defined by a satin welting. I took the dress out and held it up in front of me. As I stood up on the bed where I could see my whole figure in the dresser mirror, I swished to and fro and admired myself. I didn't hear the door open.

I turned on hearing a shriek from Katherine. "Oh my God — she's got my dress — she'll ruin it!" she screeched.

"Who let her get it? Mamma! That little Runt has my brand new dress out! With her filthy hands and legs, she'll ruin it!"

My mother hobbled to the door of the bedroom. "Oh that child would provoke a saint. She's got her nose into everything. Here, give that dress back to your sister. How in the world could you do a thing like that with your hands not washed, touching your big sister's dress? Why, you should be ashamed of yourself."

I threw the dress on the bed, jumped off and ran to the parlor. "Out, Runt," I heard Beady command, "Daddy's doing homework with me . . . so don't be sticking your nose in."

"What was you doing to get the Katrin's goat?" Pop asked.

"Nothing" I said, holding back my tears, "just looking at her old dress was all —"

I could hear Katherine bossing my mother in the other room. "It was not folded like that, Mom; I know it wasn't. It's going to be all ruined. That smudge wasn't on the front."

"Now don't be going on, Katherine," Mom soothed. "Now she didn't ruin it at all. We'll hide it someplace where she won't get it."

There was no place to go in the railroad flat. I left Beady and my father, went into my mother's and father's room, crawled under their big double bed and sat in the dark.

Jean Margaret made her first holy communion at Eastertime. Her picture was taken in the churchyard and on her front stoop with all her relatives and she got to pose in the middle, holding a bouquet of lily of the valley. Everybody made a fuss over her and wanted to stand next to her.

I couldn't get over how gorgeous she looked, all in white, so holy.

Sundays in Brooklyn were dull and boring. All the shops on Liberty Avenue were closed. Even the bakery shut its doors at noon. The El trains ran at a snail's pace.

Often Daddy had the itch to go on excursions Sunday mornings. He developed a taste for thrift shops on the Lower East Side of Manhattan. Our lives were shaped by what he happened upon. After stumbling onto language primers, he decided we'd all be multilingual. Although we never progressed beyond the counting stages, we had learned to say "Hello," "How are you?" and "I love you" in seven languages. That remained the extent of our linguistic knowledge. The quests went on. When he found ice skates in a secondhand shop, we became ice-skaters. He paid little attention to sizes; we stuffed them with newspapers or wore several layers of socks, and he took us skating in Forest Park. He bought us secondhand Chinese robes which Mom said had to be fumigated before she'd let us wear them. We had secondhand sleds, cans of lovely old beads to sort and restring, hand-painted china, outdated *National Geographic* magazines, and encyclopedias. He bought us picture books of wild flowers and birds and maps of Africa, Europe, and the Arctic Circle.

Pop insisted on taking us with him every Sunday until Beady, like Katherine before her, rebelled. So I went alone with my father to Orchard Street on the Lower East Side. He'd buy me a hot dog at Nathan's and I'd follow him to a bar, where he'd have a few beers and a hard-boiled egg or a cold potato while I'd finish my hot dog and sauerkraut. Then we'd visit the antique stalls on Ludlow Street, where Daddy, now mellowed on beer, would greet the stall owners effusively. He spoke a "little Russki to this one," "a little bit German with other fellow . . ." as we shopped.

Daddy developed a passion for music, and over the years collected a banjo, a mandolin, a harmonica, and a violin. Thus our Sunday musicals evolved, which had such elaborate preparations. There was much bobbing of the head and intense concentration on finger position when he decided on the strings. The holding and the playing of the violin seemed the most arduous. He fidgeted and fussed until he found a comfortable position for his chin. He peered out of his tortoise-shell glasses, fixed his grey eyes on the three of us, and opened and closed them in an effort to center his concentration. Then he'd sway comically from left to right, raise his eyebrows on the high notes, and lower them on the low notes. The vibratos caused a twitching in his facial expression, which usually caused one of us to giggle, and then the glaring would start. We rarely recognized the tunes he played. Every Sunday, after the midday meal, we were summoned into the parlor. Only Beady could carry a tune, but Katherine and I were expected to sing along too, sotto voce, while Daddy conducted us in song. His taste in music was catholic, so our repertoire consisted of "Oh Sole Mio" in Italian, "The Merry Widow" in Croatian, and the "Internationale" in English.

We were lined up in front of the mantelpiece one Sunday and Dad was conducting us in a songfest with lavish gestures.

> *"Arise, you prisoners of starvation,*
> *Arise, you wretched of the earth,*
> *For justice thunders condemnation —*
> *A better world's in birth."*

(The noise of the El caused us to pause and in the wait, we heard a persistent rapping on the parlor door.)

When Daddy opened it, revealing two black-frocked figures, my sisters fled through the flat to the kitchen. I remained trapped between my father and the nuns.

Daddy greeted them extravagantly. "Come in, come in," he beckoned. He ordered me to "clear the comics from the couch so ladies have place to sit."

The short fat nun perched herself in the middle of our wine-colored velvet couch. Her weight raised the dust, which floated about in the sunlight. Milky blue eyes swelled through her silver-rimmed glasses. Her face was very round and the mouth was just a slash dividing her nose and chin. She identified herself as Margaret Teresa. Her companion, tall and thin by contrast, adjusted her robes before she sat. Her long, skinny El Greco fingers deftly folded the gown into neat pleats, which then fell gracefully and protectively over her knees. She placed her hands together, palms up, in her lap and slowly raised her veiled head to meet my father's gaze. Her eyes caught the light like amber beer bottles in the sun; her black brows ran perfectly parallel to the white strip of her habit cutting across her forehead; her worm-shaped lips had a purple hue, and when she spoke her voice was hoarse and sexy. "I'm Sister Alice Marie," she said.

My father folded his arms and poised himself against the mantelpiece. I pressed into the corner near the lamp. Their presence charged our flat with more disturbance than five express trains at rush hour. I sensed some sinister mischief in my father and I realized with alarm that this Sister Alice Marie was nicknamed Sister Sam by Jean Margaret and my friends in parochial school. She had the reputation of giving kids nightmares. ("I'm telling Sister Sam" was the threat which cowed the most wicked bully into returning a stolen hat or orange-crate scooter.) Finally, Sister Margaret Teresa, producing a small black notebook, broke the silence.

"Now you are Mr. Jackson. You have a family of five, is that right?"

"I am John Jackson, head of family, that is perfectly correct."

"And your wife is a Catholic; is that right, Mr. Jackson?"

"She is Irish Catholic, correct."

Sister Margaret Teresa wet the lead point of her pencil with her tongue and waited. "What are the names and ages of the children?" she asked.

"The Katherine is seventeen; the Beatrice, or middle girl, however you wish to specify, is thirteen years, and baby is ten. Not so much baby any more."

"And all three girls were baptized, were they?"

"Yes. We went through that hocus-pocus."

Silence. Sister Alice Marie laid a quieting hand on her companion. Then she took over.

"Well, actually, Mr. Jackson, we're concerned with your girls and their religious training. Although they've all been baptized to the faith until they make that first holy communion, they can't be confirmed, and without being confirmed they can't get absolution. Should something happen to them . . ."

"Wait, wait," my father broke in. There was the hint of annoyance creeping into his voice. "You mean they can't go to the priest for confessing, is that your meaning?"

"That's exactly right, Mr. Jackson."

"Yeah, well, see . . . I don't like whole idea of confessing to stranger, calling him Father; he is not father. I am entitled to that respect. I am working to feed and clothe them. So it is my job, my obligation to punish or forgive them when they need it. Wirgin Mary is not their mother. Priest is not their father."

"Well, Mr. Jackson," Sister Alice Marie narrowed her eyes slightly and continued, "in our faith we are talking about the spiritual."

"No, no, darling," my father interrupted, "let's not get into semantics. If my children steal or lie, I do correcting. No Hail Mary's ten times, no mumbo jumbo or hitting breast and whining to priest, 'Forgive me, father, for I have sinned.'"

While the other sat in silence, Sister Margaret Teresa erupted in a fit of dry coughing, patting her mouth with quick little jerks of her hand, her eyes bulging even more behind her steel-rimmed glasses. She kept trying to apologize in staccato gasps.

"You want little schnapps?" my father asked.

"No, no," she wheezed, her face blue and her eyes red. "Please, I'm fine." Sister Sam grimly passed her a handkerchief. "Sister, are you all right now?" she asked huskily.

As a train went by the room was thrown into temporary shadow. The sounds of the El turning toward the next station faded. The coughing had stopped.

"Well, Mr. Jackson," Sister Alice Marie said, rising, about to terminate the visit, "I hope you will consider sending the girls to the parish house so that they can start learning their catechism. I could arrange for the older ones to have private sessions. This one," she said, meaning me, "is still young enough to come to regular classes."

"There's nothing to consider," my father replied with exaggerated politeness. "Why would I throw my children into den of lions? No, your profession makes you biologically unsound to handle youth. To marry church is not normal for grown people. That's unhealthy atmosphere for the young."

If Sister Alice Marie or Sister Margaret Teresa was offended, they didn't show it. They turned in unison at the door and smiled piously. They had tried to save us. Sister Alice Marie said, "We'll pray for you and your family, Mr. Jackson."

"All right," my father sang after them. "No hard feelings, girls."

He shut the door after they reached the landing at the end of the hall, and there was the flutter of black wings and the patter of their feet descending the three flights down to the street and safety.

I followed my father into the kitchen, where my mother and sisters were huddled.

"How could you make a show of yourself in front of those holy women? You've undermined me and my faith, John. These children will never be able to set foot in church again," my mother cried.

Daddy didn't answer. He reached for his cap with the green visor and summoned the three of us to follow to his garden. We had hoped when we moved to Brooklyn that our weeding days were over, but Daddy had found a vacant lot several blocks from our tenement and we walked there in silence.

Once he entered his garden, a beatific look came over his face. He hung his shirt on the corner of the grape arbor and tied a bandanna into four knots around his head. It covered that part of his pate that the visor of his cap left exposed. He stood in his sleeveless undershirt, his hands on his hips and his shoes sinking into the delicious earth. He pointed out the weeds. His fingers were knowledgeable and quick as he tugged them out and then ever so gently he caressed the earth back around the little seedlings.

He lined us up in a row and reviewed the weeding procedure.

"Here, take like this — be sure not to step on this little fellow — go to earth and grab firmly at base, then pull out parasite. See this little bastard? That's bloodsucker. He steals nourishment from the flowers. You got to be good detective, because weeds sometimes look like plants.

"That's it. Don't be afraid. Katrin, come in here where coreopsis are. Beatrice and Anna, over there where is cosmos and baby's breath. Look how delicate stem is on cosmos. Most sweet flower."

After Pop made sure we were concentrated and efficient, he went to the far end of the plot. Spade in hand and looking heavenward, his voice trailing back to us, he said quietly, "I tell you what is miracle. The nature." And with that he stamped his foot hard on the spade and lovingly turned the fresh earth for his new flower bed.

I guess most girls want to be like their mothers, but I didn't. Though as a young child I was preoccupied with winning my mother's love and attention, in adolescence I switched my allegiance to Katherine, who became my ideal. I wanted to be just like her when I grew up; she seemed the perfect "big young girl." I even named my paper dolls after her.

I remember her in pinwheel hats that matched the blue or brown in the princess-styled silk print dresses she wore. She was always very careful about how she dressed. Her slip never hung below her hemline. When she got a new frock, she'd stand on a kitchen chair as Mom circled her, pins in her mouth, to make sure the hem was perfectly straight.

Katherine squinted to see herself in the mirror over the sink.

"No, it's crooked here, hon...."

"Well, turn slowly, Katherine, so I can see," Mom directed.

After graduating from John Adams High School, Kay landed her first job, as an office clerk with Avon & Company at Radio City in New York. She had to lie on the application for the job because her high school sorority sisters warned her that if she didn't write "Protestant" where it said "religion," they might not accept her. Mom was very excited and proud of Kay and her important new job. I began to entertain romantic visions of one day commuting to and from Manhattan myself.

On my way to school in the mornings, I'd walk to the El with Katherine. She said, "Let me walk ahead, hon, so you can see if my seams are straight, O.K.?" I watched her checking those seams as she stood on one foot. How she managed to balance herself on those high-heeled ankle-strap sandals, I'll never know. She usually stopped to examine herself in the long narrow mirror outside Vinnie's shoe store next to the fruit stand. Sal the fruit guy would drop his carton of oranges and whistle when he noticed her. A handsome Sicilian with a chipped front tooth, he was forever packing or unpacking the fruit and vegetables on his stand at the corner of McKinley and Liberty avenues. He always saved the slightly bruised peaches and doled them out to us kids. But he was especially nice to me because he had a crush on Katherine. He referred to her as "dynamite" or "the chick with the Petty Girl legs."

Katherine weighed 112 pounds, was five-foot-two, had grey eyes just like Pop's, and titian hair. All the guys called her Red. They constantly vied for her attention — including Dominick, the cop. He stood in front of the butcher shop on Liberty Avenue at Grant, shaking his leg and hiking his belt self-consciously when my sister came into sight. Angelo, the butcher's son, always managed to run out in time to greet her as she ran for the morning train.

Angelo and Dominick would follow her flight with their eyes as she ran up the El steps. She flushed a lot and held one white-gloved hand onto her hat while the other clutched her skirts close.

Mr. Carbusi, Angelo's father, even got into the act. "Hey, Angelo," he yelled, loud enough to be heard over the onrushing trains, "will you stop with your girl-crazy tricks? Shake it up! We got work to do. Do you want Dominick to get sore at us? She's his girl!"

Dominick feigned a scowl of annoyance and barked, "Come on, will ya, Pop," and swaggered away. Angelo would return to the shop, tying his white apron strings tighter in the front.

I felt a little sorry for the guys and sometimes I'd get annoyed at or jealous of my sister, who kept all of her socializing outside of the neighborhood. When she graduated from John Adams, all of her beaus and even her sorority sisters came from the Ozone Park or Jamaica areas. Even after graduation she kept in touch with the same high school sorority crowd.

When she landed the job at Avon, they came to our house to celebrate. Mom preened with excitement and pride at Kay's getting that "situation" and having her "crowd over." As far as Mom was concerned, nothing was too good for my older sister. She acted toward Kay just like Grandma had with the "men" who worked. Suddenly food was put away just for her. "Don't be touching that banana . . . I'm saving it for Katherine's shredded wheat. Be sure to leave that cream on top of the milk for Kay's coffee. Don't finish all those biscuits. I want some for Kay when she comes home. Here, don't be sitting on Katherine's bed; she just put that clean bedspread on for the company."

That club meeting caused more commotion in my life than any opening night I can remember. I wasn't allowed to walk on the floors anywhere. This linoleum was just scrubbed, that floor was just polished, this rug was just carpet-swept, that mat was just shook.

"Here, drink from this jelly glass; those good glasses were just shined. Don't be going in the room" — the parlor suddenly became "the room" — "it's all been cleaned." Ashtrays were bought. Two or three of the girls smoked — Mom didn't comment on that — and I even know that Katherine had a pack of Luckies in her drawer under her ecru slip.

I was getting so nervous and so anxious myself over the endless preparations and the orders of "don't touch that ham; don't touch that bread; don't touch that cream, the butter, milk, cookies, or the nonpareils." We kids called the nonpareils "louse heads" because those little white pellets looked like nits, but we never bought them because they weren't penny candy; they were just too fancy.

Beady had her hair in curlers for two days before the party, first in sugar water and then in beer to hold the curl. It got too frizzy so she had to wash it out and start again. She kicked and cried until Mom shouted, "Why, those girls aren't coming to see you, anyway."

Beady and I both were intimidated by Mom's bragging about Kay's sorority sisters. "Why, that Dot McGinley," Mom boasted, "comes from a real fine family." Dot's father was a fireman. They lived on a quiet, tree-lined street in a refined neighborhood in Queens and owned their two-family brick house with a one-car garage. They had a privet hedge and had to water their lawn, it was so large. Geraldine (or "Gerry") Geise wasn't just well-off. "Why, her people are practically high society!" Mom said.

Then there were Jessie and Beth; they were poorer girls, Irish and very respectable and neat. "Oh my God, those girls are just bandbox clean," Mom would boast. They each wore a white sweater washed in Ivory Soap with a green T on it over a stylish skirt, pleated and short. The T was their sorority letter, which stood for Tau Tau Gamma. Some had their fellas' gold footballs on chains bouncing between their nubile breasts. They wore brown and white saddle shoes smelling of Griffin polish and their anklets, worn over their silk stockings, matched the green in the letter T. They all seemed to wear camel or tweed coats with fluffy fur collars. Every one of them wore red lipstick and flashed white, even teeth. Their hair, whistle-clean and bouncy, was shoulder-length, except for Gerry, who had a personality cut.

"Not everyone can wear her hair like that, do you think?" Kay's questions to Mom were usually rhetorical. She was laying out the cold cuts for her meeting. "But Gerry has the hair for it," she continued. "It falls right into that wave on her forehead. She looks real cute with it. And of course her head's a good shape. Now Jessie could certainly wear that, but you can't get her to cut her hair. Someone told her she looks like Ann Sheridan — and it's true. She has that thick, wavy hair; but her eyes are just beautiful . . . those big green orbs."

"Oh, she's a wonderful-looking girl," Mom said. "All those girls are fine-looking and so considerate. They always come in to see how I am. They're all so refined!"

"Oh they think you're just darling, Mom," Kay went on. Kay rubbed lemon on her fingers after finishing with arranging her cold cuts, and then, squinting at Mom, went in to her bedroom and brought out creams, lipsticks, perfumes, and hand lotions — samples she'd brought home from Avon. When she suggested that Mom should try them, my mother became shy and girlish.

"Now you know, Katherine, I don't use any paint on my face."

"You have gorgeous skin, Mom, with that beautiful Irish coloring. But you know, hon, it gets all dry and you should cream around the eyes and at the neck — that's where those little fine wrinkles start."

"Oh, you are comic, Katherine," Mom said with a giggle. "Anyone would think you had a stake in that company. Why, what will Daddy say or think if he sees you putting those things on my face?"

Nevertheless, by the time the girls arrived, Mom had put on her best navy dress and a dab of rouge on her cheeks, which brought out the blue of her eyes. Even I had a touch of powder on my freckled cheeks and nose. Katherine, out of her own money, bought me a turquoise linen dress from the Pre-Teen department at A&S. It had darts at the bust. "Wash real good, mind you, before you put that dress on," Mom had warned — "Arms, knees, neck, and elbows."

I was excited about the girls coming because I knew I would get the chance to imitate movie stars and eat the party food between my acts. Katherine had me do a whole number on Sal and Angelo. She loved showing me off, and by this time I didn't need much coaxing; I was flattered to be a part of the evening.

I knew I wanted to be an actress by the time I was six, but I never admitted it to my contemporaries. "I'm going to be a stenographer," I'd say, figuring that sounded important enough to me and it left them without comment. Coming right out and revealing my life's secret fantasy would have chanced their saying, "Boy, she thinks a lot of herself," and I wouldn't have been able to bear that. Yet somehow I also liked the idea of following in Katherine's footsteps by becoming an office girl. I wanted to have my own crowd and to swish past the guys on Liberty Avenue on my way to the El, Manhattan, and "work."

Katherine, however, whether she knew it or not, had awakened and nourished the actress in me. I'd run to her with new impersonations worked into skits of Sal at the fruit stand and Angelo and his pop at the meat market. She egged me on and set me up in front of her friends to do my showing off. In fact, she took stage in the middle of the parlor, quieting her group and describing my precociousness in detail.

"I can't go a step out this door without one of the store clerks in City Line saying, 'That kid sister of yours takes the cake. Where in the world does she get that vocabulary? She must have swallowed the dictionary.' Tell them what you said to Sal, hon," Katherine coached.

"Well," I said, "Sal walks like this and he wears gloves without fingers and a wool hat even in the summertime. And he always says, 'Hi, Annie Jane . . . how are you, sweetheart? Where's your sister? Can't you put in a good word for me with her? What is she, stuck-up? She doesn't wanna buy the fruit?'

" 'I'm the one my mother sends, Sal, because my mother is particular about our fruit, so please pick judiciously.'

" 'Jeeze, kid, where do you pick up those words? What are you gonna be, a lawyer or something?' "

The girls applauded and then I was rewarded with a little ham sandwich with the crusts cut off and a sip of orange soda. No sooner had I taken my first gulp than Kay had me up again to do my description of shopping at the butcher's.

I described how Mr. Carbussi wore a paper bag on his head, and when I came into the shop he'd dance over the sawdust floor, remove the toothpick from his mouth and give me a huge grin. "How's my favorite carrot top? Oh boy, wait 'n Angelo hears who's here. Hey Angelo, I got your favorite customer out here!"

"Who is it, Pop?" Angelo asked, a little annoyed at being interrupted while butchering in the back.

"It's your sweetheart, the Jackson girl," Mr. C. teased, winking and raising his eyebrows at me.

I mime Angelo dropping his cleaver and beginning to primp. His wiping his bloody hands on the white apron, then straightening his butcher cap with his name written on it in blue lettering. He wears a tie which I pretend to straighten, although he never did that, and I mimic his loping into the shop like Groucho Marx. Then I did his face falling in abject disappointment when he sees me instead of Kay.

"Oh, hi, kiddo," he says, and out of the side of his mouth he reprimands Mr. C. "You're very funny, Pop," he says. His father exaggerates innocence.

"What are you talking about? I thought it was your girl friend. I can't tell the two sisters apart. Well, I'll take the little one; she's my type." The old devil is relentless. Angelo shakes his head and wheezes, a sound of exasperated incredulity.

"O.K., Anna Jane, what is it today?" he asks.

"My mother wants," I pipe up in my own voice, "six pork chops, *thin* and very *lean*, Angelo. And flatten them good, my mother says."

"O.K., O.K. Whatever your mother says, she's got. How's your beautiful sister? Why doesn't she come in?"

My sister squealed with laughter, covering her blushing face with her hands as I continued, loving her reaction.

"Because she's at work," I said. "Some people have to work for their living, Angelo —" I fresh-mouthed.

"Oh yeah, yeah," Angelo says and then adds, "make sure she comes on Saturday, O.K.? She only works half day on Sat'day, right? I love you, Anna Jane, but I love your sister better — so make sure; O.K.?"

"O.K., Angelo, I'll tell my mother."

"No, don't tell your mother, dopey. Tell your sister. O.K., sweetheart?" Then I'd do Angelo's Groucho walk — which got me a round of applause, and the plate full of nonpareils.

Acting and movies began to mean the world to me in my adolescent years. Pagan though it was, the City Line movie house became my shrine. My obsession with Catholicism and its magic rituals waned; I now adored the movies and would beg, borrow, or threaten suicide for the price of admission.

Friday became my movie day. As three o'clock and the end of the school day drew near, excitement and anticipation overcame me. I experienced no greater joy than wiggling my toes and feeling the movie dime secure in my shoe. At the dismissal bell, I tore home, defying traffic, jumping mud puddles in empty lots, weaving through backyards and risking encounters with vicious barking dogs. I took the four flights of steps two at a time all the way up to our landing and crashed through the kitchen door with an ecstatic shriek, "Mother darling, I am home!"

"Here, don't be shouting at the top of your lungs like that. Go in your room and change your middy blouse. You'll need it again on Monday. Then pick us up some rye bread for Daddy's supper before you rush off to the show."

Oh, the movies! My addiction was insatiable. Because the City Line movie house couldn't supply me with films fast enough, I would often walk thirteen blocks or more to the Cross Bay or the Embassy movie house. It didn't matter that the trips home alone at night set my hair on end, the thrill of seeing a movie was worth any hardship. I'd race past the funeral parlor so fast my throat hurt and finally storm into the house, late for supper, pale as a ghost and still gasping for breath.

My mother worried about the effect movies had on me and resolved to censor my movie-going. My new wisecracking vocabulary offended her. I put steel clicks on the heels and toes of my shoes and scratched her floors with my tap-dancing antics. By this time I'd shed the image of the saintly little martyr and began to get into hair-pulling matches with Beady. I challenged her right to loll at home in hair curlers while I did all the errands and all the family marketing. I was forever being chased out of the house by either her or my mother, and made emotional exits, slamming doors after melodramatic speeches. "You'll right this wrong you've done me, Mother dear." "I'm in bondage to no man. Do you hear me, Beatrice Jackson?!" "You're not worth my breath." "I'll never again give a sucker an even break!"

Beady gloated as Mom flew into rages. Her warning would pursue me through the dark halls: "Your father will hear of this when he gets home, Lady Jane. You'll not set foot in this house till you repent."

I headed for the street in an agony of rage and sought

solace on the long stone steps beside the City Line (re-named the Earl Theatre by its new owner). There was a crack in the side doors I could look through and see the movie. Even though the head of one of my idols was flat-tened out like pie dough and his eyes and nose went sliding out of view, the voices and dialogue soothed my strained nerves.

As it became harder and harder for me to extract my movie dime from Mom, I connived and found other ways of scraping up the fare.

One solution was to go fishing in the cellar grates, but this was chancy, time-consuming, and involved an invest-ment of two or three cents for bubble gum. Chewed to the right consistency, the gum was stuck on the end of an old mop or broom handle and placed between the grate slats. When my eyes adjusted to the darkness in the storm sewer, I stirred around the debris of candy wrappers, apple cores, bottle caps and old wet leaves until I uncovered a penny, nickle, or maybe even a dime; never more than that.

The drugstore grate by the El station was the most popular grate-fishing spot. All the shoeshine boys, from whom I learned this lucrative technique, hung out there. They resented my fishing in their grate and would harass me as I poked about by standing in my light, kicking my elbows, and making me nervous enough to drop my coin midway up. Finally I learned to pay them off.

The record yield for grate-fishing was twenty-six cents. But when such a sum was found, there was always the dan-ger of a gold rush. Kids from all over the neighborhood, as far away as Ozone Park and across Sunset Boulevard, came with broomsticks and bubble gum.

When Katherine saw me lying on my belly with my nose between the iron slats, she reported my activities to my mother, who then forbade me to disgrace the family any-

more. Daddy, when told, didn't like the mercenary aspects
of it, so I embarked upon the arduous enterprise of collecting silver foil, making it into a ball and then selling it to the
junk man. This meant weeks of scouring the gutters for
old cigarette packs, not to mention the consummate skill, as
well as time, involved in separating the foil from its white
paper linings. This venture went up in smoke, too, when I
tried to glue the foil onto a pair of old summer shorts in an
effort to convert them into the dazzling silvery ones I'd seen
on Eleanor Powell. When I tried to wear them, they fell
apart; I couldn't even rescue the foil for the junk man.

Bottle deposits were another source for movie money,
but our family never had more than eight milk bottles in a
week. At two cents a bottle, that was at best sixteen cents,
and I had to split that with Beady for her bank. I used to go
to the store for people, wheel babies about for hours, or
walk along streets, my eyes fixed on the pavement, hoping
to find something. The goal was always the movies.

The hardest and most wearing way to get that dime
was begging and fighting Mom for it. The incident which
keeps surfacing in my mind had to do with Jean Harlow's
film *Saratoga,* which I battled to see. The seeds of that war
of wills with my mother were sown the June day Harlow
died. That day I went for Mom's *Daily News* and saw the
picture of Jean Harlow smiling on the upside-down paper,
her platinum hair spread over the entire front page. I kept
turning the paper around so I could study her face from all
angles. There were photographs all over the centerfold, of
her in gorgeous satin gowns and some of her in white fox.

I couldn't wait to break the news and was announcing
it in the hallway on the last flight up.

"Guess who died?" I shouted, before showing Mom
the headline.

"My God in heaven," she said. "Here, let me see that. My God, my God," she shook her head in disbelief.

I told her that people were saying Jean Harlow's brain was poisoned from all the hair dye. "Well, I wouldn't doubt that for a minute. It goes to show you, no matter how much money you have or how famous you become, you pay the price like anyone else. Well, she's gone now, so there's no use talking against her."

She studied Harlow's pictures in the centerfold.

"She didn't have a lick on under those satin dresses. It was disgraceful; you could see everything she owned." Her voice became contemplative. "A young woman like that . . . They say William Powell was madly in love with her. He was going to marry her, they say. She was divorced, too, which is why the Legion of Decency banned her pictures from us Catholics."

I now wanted to see that movie on two counts — because it was banned and because I was intrigued with the idea of a double who would look and talk like Harlow finishing the movie.

Almost daily the papers were flooded with news of the progress of *Saratoga,* which Harlow was acting in at the time of her death. When it finally played at the Cross Bay, I asked my mother for a dime.

"Why, you were just at the show on Friday," she said.

"The picture changed. I have to see Jean Harlow."

"Well, I don't have a dime for you to squander. It's sinful what they show, anyway."

"Please, please, please, Mamma." I dropped to my scabbed knees and clasped my hands in prayer. "I beg of you on my mercy." I clutched her skirt and crawled after her. "I'll never be bad again."

My mother whacked me on the head with the damp dishtowel.

"Get up off the floor this minute, you little rip. You're not going, so you can stop all this right now. When your father comes home . . . ," she threatened.

"But I want to see her and Clark Gable. It's her last movie, don't you understand? I have to see if I can tell her from her double. Oh please, please. I'm begging you on my hands and knees."

"I said no. I can put that dime to better use for milk or bananas. I'll not have you sitting ruining your eyes and corrupting your morals. You see things that aren't fit for a girl your age."

"Well, then, I'll go to the Embassy and see Myrna Loy," I lied. Mom liked Myrna Loy because she looked like our relatives. "Oh Mamma, please, Mamma. I'll do anything."

"I'll tell you what you'll do; you'll leave this house this minute or I'll get the broom to you."

"But you swore I could go if I went to Cushman's and if I went to the post office. You're breaking your solemn vow. You're a liar."

"You stop sassing me. You ought to be ashamed talking to your mother like that."

"You're not my mother; you're mean. I hate you!" I screamed.

"You. can just stop making a scene, Anna. I'm not giving in to you."

"But you practically swore on the Bible," I insisted. "If you don't let me go," I said breathing hard and changing tactics, "I'll kill myself." I grabbed the paring knife from the stove and said with such conviction that I scared myself, "You'll be sorry, Mother dear."

"Good riddance to bad rubbish," Mom returned to her scrub board.

"I hate you," I screamed, throwing myself prostrate on the linoleum floor. "I'm telling Daddy that you lied; just see if I don't."

This sent my mother to the corner for her broom. She began flying it madly. She caught my shins and sent me squealing.

"Now you get up off that floor this minute." She stood over me, her broomstick poised above her head ready for another attack. The sun lit her hair a fiery red. She looked like a Fury staring down at me.

I clasped my arms around her knees. "I beg of you on my mercy," I pleaded again. "Mamma, pleee-se," I screamed at the top of my lungs. And then we heard Mrs. MacIntyre shout and slam her door in anger. It stopped us both cold.

"Now see what you've done," Mom whispered. She returned the broom to its corner, her rage diffused. She tiptoed to her chair by the ironing board and sat.

"Now you've got the neighbors alarmed, and her girls just got over scarlet fever. . . . I could die of shame," she said and began crying. "Oh, I just hope you have children who abuse you the way you abuse me. As true as God's in heaven, you'll be punished for this. Since the day you were born, I've had nothing but misery. I almost died when I had you and if it wasn't for you, I wouldn't have this bad leg."

The guilt and hurt from this sent me fleeing. I flung myself on the bed and buried my face in my pillow. As I heaved and sobbed and gasped for breath, emotions stirred through my body and vengeance built. In a blind rage of self-pity, I made a desperate decision to run through the kitchen and jump out the window. I wrote a hurried suicide note and off I went on my tangent. I dropped the note on the table near my mother and swung a leg out the window. "You'll be rid of me now."

"You close that window this minute. You'll have the people across the way after you next," she said in alarm as she shook soapsuds from her hands. Her fingers were all water-wrinkled. "My God, what will the neighbors think? Don't you dare do a thing like that again." Sheer panic shook her voice.

Her face paled and I watched her carefully to make sure I had gotten the proper response. But my hurt was not yet assuaged. I pulled my leg in and slammed down the window.

Mom caught me and grabbed my face in her wet, soapy hand. She squeezed my cheeks till my lips went oval, and hissed, "I never wanted you, you little bitch. You've been a trial to me since the day you were born."

"I never loved you either," I said as evenly as I could, steadying my voice. "You're mean and cruel and I wish you were dead." We stood in silence, eyeing each other, and then Mom screeched, "Get out of my sight. Get out. I don't want to see you." She jerked my arm and pushed me toward the bedroom. Bitterly hurt and vengeful, I was determined to make her sorry. I took a needle from the pin cushion on the dresser and began to stab at my thumb until I drew blood, then ran my thumb over my top lip to simulate a bloody nose. I was amazed at the rich source I got from one little stab. From the other room, I could hear Mom open the window to hang out her wash.

I dropped noisily on a chair near the sink in the kitchen so she would be sure to catch sight of me. She went about her business silently, her mouth pulled tight in anger as she twisted the water out of my dress. With one leg up on the chair, I was examining my swollen shin, feigning bravery, wincing just loud enough to wrest some attention from her. I felt her looking.

"Put your leg down; you're getting too big to be sitting like that."

Obediently, I put my leg down, and I pulled my dress taut over my knees modestly. I looked up at her, giving her a view of my face.

"What's happened to your nose?" she asked, frowning.

"I don't know," I said innocently. "Why?"

"Well, your nose is bleeding. Here, go get a wash cloth and wash it off."

I pulled my chair over to the sink. All the mirrors in our house were hung too high for me to see in. My bloody nose looked so good, I really hated to wash it. I began to believe my own lie as I gingerly cleaned the blood from my lip.

"When did you do that?" my mother asked.

"I guess it happened when you hit me," I said matter-of-factly and as kindly as I could.

Mom went back to her clothes hanging. She put the pins into her mouth. They stuck out comically on either side of her face like walrus tusks. Through the mirror I saw her drop my plaid dress onto the roof below. She stood staring for a moment, then she closed the window slowly. "You'll have to climb down," she said, shaking her head. "Oh, I don't know why you provoke me so, Anna. When you come up, you can take back those bottles under the sink."

There were only two bottles. "Couldn't I see if Beady has any money in her bank?" I asked.

"Oh my God," Mom said. "Don't go near her things or there will be the devil to pay. I don't want to stir her up."

"Well, I'll ask Mrs. I. when I go for my dress. Maybe she'll need something from the store." It embarrassed me to ask her because she had given me a nickel the day before and I had spent it on a Dixie Cup for my flip-card collection. I was ashamed to have her see me now, but it was my only chance. So I washed my face well with cold water — otherwise my eyes and nose would betray me. I grabbed my mother around the waist and begged her forgiveness.

"Well, I didn't mean what I said, either," Mom said shakily. "Now go on with you before it gets late."

I left the bottles on the landing under the stairs and braced myself to knock at Mrs. I.'s door. She called from the front room and I heard her coming through to the kitchen. I felt more comfortable because if she had been sitting vigil at the window, leaning on her red pillow, she'd probably missed hearing our fighting. I climbed out to her fire escape and got my dress. I asked her if she needed anything from the store. She said she didn't, so I had to ask red-faced and humiliated if she had any bottles for me to take back for her.

She laughed self-consciously. "What, do ya wanna go to the movies, Anna Jane?"

I nodded.

"How many bottles ya need?" she asked.

"Just three," I said. "Mom has two for me."

"You can have my Coke bottles, then. What movie you gonna see?"

"*Saratoga,*" I said, dying to leave.

"Oh yeah? What do you wanna see her for? She's dead."

"That's why I wanna see her last picture and her double." It was agony getting away from Mrs. I. I knew she was lonesome and I hated myself for wanting to leave, but my movie addiction made me callous.

I was exhausted and in low spirits as I finally set out for the movies. Reruns of the fight with my mother kept erupting in my head as I walked the several miles to the Cross Bay Boulevard and then to the island where the theatre was. Traffic whizzed around it at a dizzying speed, and my foot impatiently advanced and retreated until the light gave me the go-ahead. Heart in mouth, fingers crossed, I raced to the ticket booth. The green ticket shot out of the silver slit and I grabbed for it anxiously. Hadn't I earned it with my sweat and blood?

When the white-gloved hand of the uniformed ticket taker said, "Down front, to the matron, kid," I bristled ever so slightly at him referring to me as a child, and then raced down the aisle.

I don't remember much about *Saratoga* except a feeling of remorse and disappointment. The double was shot from the back and at quite a distance; my screaming tantrum and fight with Mom was really not worth it.

The walk home was a far worse ordeal. There was a long walk under the El's dark and ominous shadows, three or four vacant stores and, horror of horrors, the stone wall of the cemetery starting high and grading lower. An occasional light from the El train above reflected the iron gates with the star of David and made the tombstones with the Hebrew writing visible. I kept thinking I saw Jean Harlow rise behind the stones.

Somehow in my mind the whole issue of death became a dialectical dilemma. When my cousin Minnie had died, Mom said, "God takes soonest those he loveth best." When Jean Harlow died, she was being punished, for she had broken the Commandments. I decided that if I wanted to live, I'd better neither court God's favor too much nor displease him. I'd just kind of make myself small, like you do in school when you don't know the answer. You don't wave your hand or sink down in your seat. You just lower your eyes. If you don't call attention to yourself, you'll slip through unnoticed.

So I made myself a promise: I'd try with all my might and main to stop provoking my mother. Though that night I said my rosary twice through, my bad conscience about our quarrel still was not clear. As I lay in bed, my heart raced so that I could hardly breathe. I was sure I was dying and I was too ashamed to ask God for everlasting life.

But within the week, I was myself again and my movie madness returned as strong as ever.

My infatuation with movies wasn't limited just to viewing; I loved to act. After seeing a Sonja Henie movie, I was at my worst. If she was the Pavlova of the ice, I was hell bent on being "Queen of Ball Bearings." I shortened all my skirts, wore a white Swiss-style sweater with green pom-poms, and had a red embroidered cap tied under my chin. I could hardly contain my excitement until I got my skates strapped on and could race through the streets trying fancy stops, toe-dancing, and spins.

I skated up and down hills and even jumped the steps in Forest Park. I skated backward from Lincoln Avenue, around to McKinley Avenue, back down to Forbell Street, then careened up to Liberty Avenue, paralleling the trolley tracks. My shoes became scruffed and torn from the bite of the skate clamps. My fourth toe spasmed; I wore out wheels, sparks flew; the steel on my skates wore thin and snapped, leaving me to wobble along on two discs. Still I persevered, and no amount of scolding from my mother would deter me. I spreadeagled around the iron sewer covers, outstretched my arms and balanced on one leg until suddenly the insistent beep of a horn and a yell from the driver interrupted me — "Hey kid . . . get the hell out of the street before you get your ass knocked off!" — and tore me out of my Technicolor reverie.

After that I returned to the sidewalks again and took to hanging around the old City Line movie house. I'd wait around until the first feature ended and then sneak in, making sure the second feature was a movie I had already seen, because I couldn't bear the thought of being turned out in the middle of a new film. Having memorized my favorite movies down to the last word of dialogue, I'd act them out in their entirety for the crowds that gathered on the Lincoln Avenue stoops. My rendition of *San Francisco* drew a standing-room-only crowd. I was quite an expert at getting laughs.

Performing in front of a live audience had become vital to me. At home I practiced with Beady, but she was more competitor than audience. She was a great mimic herself, and I honed and sharpened my observations on her criticisms. We played the game of "Who's This?" imitating friends, relatives, and movie stars, arguing and correcting each other's interpretations. No movie star of the mid-thirties and early forties went unnoticed by us. I won my sister's undying admiration by impersonating Henry Armetta in a scene with Alice Faye and John Payne. My walk of Armetta, spinning his tray and greeting the lovebirds in his restaurant, sent Beady into convulsive laughter and made her so envious that we had to switch to her favorite game, "Singing Every Song in the World."

When our big radio broke down, depriving us of our

favorite radio shows — "The Fred Allen Show," "The Lone Ranger," "The Little Theater off Times Square," and "Major Bowes' Amateur Night" — Beady got her lists and music sheets out from under the clock on the mantel and announced that we would take turns crouching inside the broken radio. Of course, she went first because she invented the game.

"Turn me on," she commanded, and then she'd start imitating various singers. She was always trying to fool me with her exotic choices.

"That's Wee Bonnie Baker; that's Lily Pons," I'd guess.

"Wrong," Beady said, interrupting her operatic aria from *The Great Waltz*. I went crazy trying to guess. "It's Miliza Korjus," Beady said triumphantly. Finally, Mom put a stop to it.

"You've school tomorrow, and I can't stand much more of that screeching in there."

When I didn't have Beady to perform with, I stood on the rung of my bed and play-acted in front of the large oval mirror. I saw neither straight red hair nor freckles; I saw Irene Dunne in *Magnificent Obsession*. I was so convincing in this role that I even made myself cry. But I was humiliated when Beady caught me at my act. "I'm telling Mom you put her powder on. I'm telling Kay you've been playing with her brassiere. And I'm telling Daddy you smoked his cigarettes." She grabbed my hair, pulled it rudely, and said, "Give me back my barrette," or "Take my curlers out of your ugly hair this minute."

"They're not yours; they're Kay's," I cried.

"They're mine when she's not using them." Then the kicking and the cat-fighting would start and Mom would intercede with the broom.

Fights over the curlers became more frequent as I took to imitating movie stars' hairdos. Today's pompom was incorporated into tomorrow's upsweep. When I fell in love with Laurence Olivier as Heathcliffe, I shaved my hair line for a Merle Oberon effect. The result was ghastly — even I saw that — so I had to adapt a Veronica Lake one-eyed look.

When Judy Garland became popular, I developed a lisp; but it was seeing Eleanor Powell tap dance on a typewriter that charged me with a new enthusiasm. I went all out for tap-dancing. I began to hang around Valetta's dancing school, where Katherine took a Thursday night class. I had another good excuse to haunt the studio — Daddy worked in the barber shop next door and beneath Valetta's, which was eye-level with the El. Every passing El train stopped at the station and people would stare in at Valetta's, and even applaud the dancers in their cute little shorts. But Valetta trained her dancers not to notice their captive audience. When the weather was mild, the side windows were opened and someone standing on the street could look up and see twenty legs kicking and turning synchronously, or hear the rhythmic taps, shuffle-step, shuffle-step, shuffle-stepping away.

My friend Eileen McGirney was the star pupil at Valetta's in tap, toe, and acrobatics. Her mother cleaned and polished the studio floors to help pay for her lessons and Valetta sprung for her gorgeous costumes. Eileen never showed off, though, and she'd never wear her costumes on the street unless they could be hidden under a coat. Her constraint was as much from modesty as from professionalism. I was so impressed by Eileen's brilliant dancing that when I saw her flip through the air — a blur of feathers dizzily spinning — I was tongue-tied with admiration.

I ached to be a part of that world. There was just no use thinking about it, though, because lessons cost fifty cents each, and I had no shoes of my own. Even if I could have gotten my hands on Kay's tap shoes, there was just no way of keeping them on my feet. The only thing I could do was practice tap-dancing in my oxfords on the street in front of McGirney's stoop with Dolly, Eileen's younger sister.

But neither my street dancing career nor my brief exposure to the stage as the Spirit of Thanksgiving in a fourth grade play was enough for me. I had dreams about Clark Gable, Gary Cooper, and Laurence Olivier. If only I would get discovered, I fantasized, I could wear satin gowns with fox on the sleeves and fur on the bottom, and talk fresh to the heroes. Then one day it happened.

I skated into the life of Walter Heinz, my first real contact with show business, in the spring of 1937, when I was going on twelve years old. Walter was the handsome new manager of the City Line movie house. He wore yellow shirts and cravat ties, snazzy sport coats, well-fitted and well-pressed, and impeccably creased grey flannel slacks.

The moment I saw Walter, I fell for him. He had that Hollywood look: perfectly tailored clothes, tanned face, smoky grey eyes, and finely chiseled profile. His voice had a metallic ring to it, and his accent was western and different. He threw back his head when he laughed and crinkled his forehead, closing his eyes in a sweet agony of laughter. Oh, he was gorgeous!

After meeting him, I dropped the boys who hung out at the candy store. It no longer thrilled me to skate and be grabbed by them now that I had Walter, who was actually friendly with movie stars. He knew Isabel Jewel in person. (I was only mildly impressed by that.) When he became manager of the City Line, he renamed it "The Earl." The lights got brighter; the theatre was properly fumigated, and there were no more ushers running down the aisles with spray guns to rid the place of odors. Walter installed new seats and new carpets. He even put up a gold satin curtain which, when he fanned it open, reflected a gorgeous rainbow of lights. Soft organ music played in the background and created an enthralling atmosphere.

Unfortunately, he also installed a matron, but even she couldn't dim the glamour he brought to that dinky movie house, which in turn spread to the whole awful neighborhood. I lurked around that movie house for weeks before I got Walter to pay attention to me. I was already "in" with the cashier. I had whizzed by her on my roller skates one afternoon when things were slow, and we became friendly.

"Hi, Anna Jane . . . what's up, kid?" she asked. "Hey, wanna get me a Coke by the candy store? There's two cents for ices in it for you."

I had to cross the trolley tracks to go to the candy store. Cobblestones lay between the rails, making it a hazardous trip on skates. I had to hold the paper cup of lemon ice between my teeth and carry the cold Coke bottle in both hands. My lip was practically frozen by the time I got back to the cashier's box. Mr. Heinz, or Walter, as I soon called him, was taking some fresh air out front.

"Don't you ever go home, kid?" he asked.

I kept at a distance on my skates and just shook my head.

"Come over here," he said and pointed to a spot in front of him. He was smiling, leaning on his new green car.

I slid over and stopped myself on my toes. It was a

terrific maneuver; I ran right into him and almost knocked him down. He balanced me and said, "Whoa, kid . . . take it easy." And we started to talk away. I had quite a mouth on me and loved showing off. I bandied phrases like "Well, that's insipid. . . ." or "How pathetic can you get?" I tried some of them out on Walter, but he was more amused than impressed — he seemed to get my number right away. As I felt more and more comfortable, I did a few imitations for him. First I did Lizzy, his platinum blonde cashier. I had her down pat. Then I moved on to Angelo the butcher. For a finale, I did my French teacher. I told him jokes and I read him my poetry. All the while I was thinking of the talent contest. Walter had begun a series of amateur nights at the Earl after the nine o'clock show on Saturday, and anyone could perform. The only hitch was that children could not go to the movies after six o'clock unless accompanied by an adult, and I knew that was a serious obstacle to my plan to win the contest. I begged Walter to let me enter the competition without the necessary adult chaperone, and finally he consented.

I knew I could win first prize if I had a gimmick. So I roller-skated over to Eileen McGirney's house with my proposal for our act. Mrs. McGirney answered the door. The family was seated at the supper table, but they invited me in anyway.

"How much do you win, if you win?" Eileen asked.

"Three dollars," I said, "and we split it."

"I should think so," Mrs. McG. said, lifting half a lip in a sneer. I always thought she had the coloring and personality of rusty metal. Her eyes were brandy brown and she combed her hair back like Garbo in *Queen Christina* and fixed it with a tortoise-shell comb. She reeked sarcasm and good-natured ridicule. On hearing my plan, she said, shaking her head and sneering again, "Well, jeeze . . . you might as well use that mouthpiece on the stage, Anna Jane. You have to be seen to be believed."

After feverish rehearsal Eileen and I were ready for our Saturday Night debut. I cast us as Dead End kids. The act began with me on stage, selling newspapers, wearing a shabby green skirt with patches and a tight-fitting peach-colored turtleneck. Eileen entered in her blue satin military costume, did a tap dance and then said to me, "Hey, what's the news on this happy July Fourth?" (That line justified her military costume.)

"Well," I replied, looking over my newspaper, "I see where this actress killed herself, but the one who went on for her was great." I then did a Katharine Hepburn from *Stage Door.*

"Oh wow!" Eileen said, "That's great." Then she launched into a buck-and-wing, leaving me to continue my routine.

"Paper . . . paper, did you hear about the mutiny?" This was my feed for Charles Laughton as Captain Bligh. I also imitated him in *Les Misérables,* which I pronounced "Less Miserables . . . ," but no one in Brooklyn knew French, so it didn't get a laugh.

Eileen then flipped through the air while I continued my Disaster Barks of "Hurricane in San Francisco . . . read all about it." Then I imitated Jack Holt discovering Jeanette MacDonald, Jeanette auditioning for Clark Gable; Spencer Tracy as the priest telling Mary (Jeanette Mac-Donald) what a good "Ave Maria" she sang. I ended with Shirley Temple and James Dunn in a scene from *Bright Eyes.* Eileen flipped once more through the applause as I exited, shouting, "Paper, paper . . . read all about the results of the amateur night at the Earl."

We were a smashing success and won the contest hands down. The news of our victory spread throughout City Line. I was invited to do my act at the beer hall on Crescent Street and to recite poetry at the Protestant church on Eldert's Lane. Walter, who became my show business advisor, alerted me of my lisp and instructed me to "drop it." He shook his head when I painted my lips vampire purple — "Get rid of those black brows, too, Annie; they don't go with your red hair. Don't rush, kid. . . . Broadway will still be there."

The thrill of a live audience pushed Hollywood and the movies into the realm of child's play. Anyway, it was a shorter trip from Brooklyn to Broadway. And that was where I was headed — *sans* roller skates.

Even my acting offered me little relief from Brooklyn's sweltering summer days. School was out, my friends would go on holidays, and the days seemed to stretch on forever. July was always a hard month for me. After the Fourth there was nothing to look forward to except the iceman. He came at exactly 11 A.M. every day; you could set your watch by him. When his truck turned into Lincoln Avenue, all the kids on the block jumped from their stoops and came running. Sometimes he chipped the ice for us, but usually he left the pick sticking in a block, knowing we'd hack off our own corners. We wrapped our chunks in newspaper so our fingers wouldn't freeze, and we sucked it till it melted.

All my friends were out by 11 A.M. waiting for the ice truck. I sometimes turned the corner with the truck and raced to get to it first. But on this particular day there wasn't a soul around. I climbed stoop after stoop in search of my friends. I rang Virginia's bell first. Her father worked nights, so he was at home during the day. He buzzed me in and as soon as I opened the downstairs door a crack, he yelled down, "Yeah?"

"Me, Mr. Harmer. Is Virginia coming down?" I called.

"Her mother took her to Howard's Bay," he yelled from the landing and then I heard his door slam.

When I leaned over the iron rail of Caroline's stoop and knocked on her window, I saw her Uncle Al sitting and listening to the radio with a fan blowing on him. He didn't even bother to get up. He just said, "Out. She's out. Her mother took the gang to Rockaway."

Mrs. Mumford was scrubbing Dotsy and Jean Margaret's hallway. "Stay off my floor, kid," she ordered, "till she dries." I kept on the other side of the bucket, which she was using as a doorstop. "I just wanted to call for Jean Margaret or Dotsy," I said.

"They all went to Coney Island Beach, which is where I shoulda took myself on a scorcher like this." She ran her mop toward me and I left, feeling dejected, rejected, and hot. I ambled down the deserted street, not even bothering to stop at the ice truck. It wouldn't have done any good anyway. Lester, the iceman, had taken his pick because nobody was around. I went into my own dark hallway and listlessly climbed the stairs.

Our hall had just been mopped, too, by the old man on the first floor, and even though it smelled of C.N. it felt cool and I knew I wouldn't get chased out. Nobody was at home but my mother. Beatrice had left early to go to her girlfriend's house. Katherine was at work in New York City and Daddy was at the barbershop on Liberty Avenue.

The neighbors downstairs were old and childless and were always quiet. They drank a lot of beer. The girls next door to us were out, too. Everybody had made plans to go places, it seemed.

My mother was emptying the ice pan when I pushed through our kitchen door. Her face was all red and blotchy from the heat. The dishrag was airing on the clothesline. "I hang it there for the sun to sweeten," she explained.

I plopped into a chair across the room from my mother. The sole of my sandal was detached.

"You'll have to leave it for Daddy to glue when he gets home if it's not too late," she said, her voice drawling in the heat. We sat in silence together. Then I got up and went to drink from the spigot. I let the water run down the side of my cheek and into my ear.

"It must be close to a hundred today," she said, "but I guess it's cooler in here than it is out there, otherwise you wouldn't come in."

"I have nobody to play with," I said. "Everybody went to Coney Island with their mother except me."

Mom looked at me for a long moment, and I suddenly read in her eyes that I had made her pity me.

"Would you like me to take you to Coney Island?" she asked.

I was so surprised and thrilled, I must have leaped up from the chair. I could feel the burn on my thighs because my damp skin had stuck to its painted surface.

Mom said, "I'll go in and dress while you wash up. Try not to splash the floor, but do your neck and wear your good shoes from under the bed."

Our trip to Coney Island together wasn't all that I anticipated because Mom wouldn't ride the Cyclone or the roller coaster or the bumper cars with me. But she wore her crepe silk dress and felt hat and rode on the merry-go-round in a bench seat. I was given an inside horse near her, but to my delight it went up and down to the music. We ordered ice cream cones — she liked vanilla the best, where I preferred tutti-frutti. Mom removed her white gloves to eat the melting cone.

I cherish this memory because it was such an unusual thing for my mother to do. She came through for me on that hot July day and I loved her for it.

Our relationship seemed to improve after this excursion. For the next couple of years I became much more considerate of my mother. I volunteered to help with housework — doing dishes, sweeping the floor, taking down garbage — and also sought her help with my lessons, for, although she was no help to me in math or history, her spelling was excellent. I treasure what tender memories I have of her from my adolescence, for when I was fourteen, she drifted into her own world one day and soon was lost to me forever.

I came home jubilant one afternoon out of bright sunlight into the dark hallway of our tenement. The temporary blindness made it difficult for me to see down the long narrow passageway. I felt apprehensive about passing that alcove next to the cellar door at the foot of the staircase: strangers were known to relieve themselves there from time to time. But it wasn't just fear that day that sent me bounding up to the first floor landing toward the light.

I was aglow with some happy tidings and wanted to share it. I might just have seen a romantic movie or been given a ride home on a boy's bike. Just the anticipation of spinning up Eldert's Lane on Richie Mahoney's handlebars and feeling the wind ballooning out my summer skirt was enough to make me soar. Whatever the reason, my spirits were high and I took the steps two at a time to the second floor landing. The super had recently cleaned; wet strings from his mop coiled around the rail slats like flat grey worms, and the strong smell of C.N. burned my throat and my nostrils.

I paused in the shaft of light streaming down from the wire-meshed skylight transom. That heavenly spotlight always brought out the actress in me and I assumed a ladylike decorum as I proceeded up to our landing, passed the hall toilet and into our kitchen, where afternoon sunlight flooded through the open windows and flickered in a rosy pattern on the worn linoleum floor.

When I entered, my mother was standing at the cupboard with her back to me wearing a print housedress of tiny orange and brown dots. Her skirt was crinkled up in back from the heat and too much starch. I could see the roll of her stocking above the knee and a pale network of blue veins on her chalk-white skin. The crown of her house slipper was crushed down by the weight of her sore foot.

I greeted her effusively and she whirled around, ordering me, "Bolt that door, Anna, I don't want that old thing forcing his attentions on me."

"Who, Mama?" I asked, taken aback.

My mother gave me a sly look but didn't answer. Instead, she stood in the doorway to the bedroom, fixing her attention on the parlor windows.

It was the quiet hour. Four o'clock street sounds wafted into the kitchen. Though the voices were faint and far away, I could distinguish the call of the huckster selling fruit from the screeches of the boys racing their orange-crate skateboards on Lincoln Avenue. I was anxious to join them, but was caught short by details I couldn't understand.

The ironing board was still up, balanced between two kitchen chairs. The clothes were dried in shapes of loaves on the table. The breakfast dishes hadn't been washed. Bits of shredded wheat clung to the cereal bowls. A coating of milk and a mound of brown banana congealed at the bottom of a dish.

The ice pan was overflowing. A stream of water was spreading out and about to crawl under the crack in the linoleum where the sunlight danced. The disarray could not be the result of the "ungodly heat." My mother never neglected her duties or her appearance.

"Shall I empty the ice pan, Mom?" I asked. I noticed the little comb that usually held her hair in place dangling at her neck. The back was pillow-matted. Obviously, she hadn't groomed herself since waking. As I crossed to the sink, balancing the round pan, my mother yelled through the rooms, directing her voice down to Liberty Avenue, "Go on with you. I'm a decent woman; don't you dare call me filthy names."

I spilled the ice water into my shoe. Mom took no notice. Her attention was riveted on phantom voices. "Who are you talking to, Mama?" I asked. My attempt at acting normal with her seemed to provoke her more.

"Don't pretend with me, Lady Jane. You know very well what those people are saying about me."

"What people, Mama?" I asked. I ran to the parlor windows and looked out, reassuring her as I hurried back to the kitchen, "My right hand up to God, Mama, there's no one down there. May God strike me dead if I'm lying," I said, and gestured.

"Oh, stop acting foolish, Anna," she said, "I'm not crazy and I'm not imagining things. You know they're there but you won't let on."

She sat down and opened her daily newspaper to the centerfold but stared beyond the pictures. She retreated into her own sphere. I went to my room and changed my shoes and socks, pulled my roller skates out from under my bed, grabbed a banana from the bowl, and headed for the street.

Mom didn't look up at all. Nor did she warn me about being home on the dot of six for supper. There was no mention of skating on the sidewalk and looking out for the cars. I was so anxious to leave, I didn't even kiss her good-bye. I felt too uneasy and estranged.

I heard her bolt the door behind me when I left. Mr. Helmsdorf passed me on the first floor landing, carrying home a quart bucket of beer.

It was well after six that Wednesday evening when Pop came, hoe in hand (he always gardened for a few hours after work when the weather was right), to summon me home. I was last on the line of skaters in a thrilling and hazardous game of whip-the-lash. We formed a chain of skaters and when we gained momentum, the leader turned, swinging the last skater around the sewer plate at dizzying speed. We were just starting to roll when Pop called. "It's your old man, Anna Jane," the leader yelled and I dropped off the whip and raced to my father.

When we turned into Liberty Avenue, we saw a crowd gathered near our doorway. Some people were looking up at our parlor windows and some were laughing nervously. Two policemen were waiting, Frank and Joey. They both knew me and Pop. Frank had an eye for my sister Katherine. "Your daughter just went up to your wife, Mr. Jackson," Frank said as we approached him, blushing as he spoke.

"What is trouble?" I heard Pop ask. For the first time in my life, I knew my father was scared.

"It's your wife, Mr. Jackson," Frank said. "She's been

yelling out the window and talking off her head for the last couple of hours since I came on duty. I think maybe you should call an ambulance and have them look her over at Queen's County or Bellevue. She might do violence to herself."

We could hear my mother screaming as we climbed the stairs; I was still wearing my roller skates.

Beady was huddled on a chair near the window, her face blotchy and red from crying. Katherine was trying to quiet my mother in the bedroom. "Now, Mama, nobody thinks any such thing," she was saying; "you're just imagining things."

I skated over the linoleum and sat in the chair next to Beady while Daddy went into the bedroom. He was wearing his undershirt and his green visor. His shoes had garden mud stuck to them, but Mom didn't notice. Katherine came out to the kitchen. We could hear Daddy try to reason with my mother. Her voice was high and out of control.

"You'll not get what you're after here, you filthy vile-mouthed things. The police are here to lock you up! Oh John," she whimpered, "those people are saying the most awful things about us. They better keep their foul thoughts to themselves."

We heard only mumbling for a time. Then Pop came back to the kitchen with his mouth pulled tight. He and Frank went into a huddle. Pop was standing looking down at his shoe, shaking his head as Frank was advising him. We only heard fragments, "Better for all concerned . . . I'd send her tonight . . . disturbing the peace . . . when they start like this . . ." Then Pop gave Katherine instructions, "Go with the sisters to Mother and get her dressed for go to hospital."

Frank and my father left to make arrangements for an ambulance. The other cop, Joey, stayed. Nobody knew how to behave. He went and looked out the kitchen window.

I unclamped my skates and on wobbly legs, I followed my sisters into Mom's room. Katherine closed the doors on either end and turned on the overhead light, which was never turned on except in winter. But everything was unusual today. Mom was sitting on her bed, looking frightened and trapped.

"Sweety," Katherine said, "Daddy wants me to help you get dressed. He's going to take you to a doctor."

"Why? There's nothing in this world wrong with me. I'm staying right here."

"Well, let's put clean clothes on anyway, hon, because Pop thinks it's best."

"He's up to no good, that father of yours. He wants to get rid of me so he can run around with those no-good women of his."

I was standing in the doorway and Mom caught me staring at her. Katherine had just lifted her housedress over her head and my mother was naked except for her step-ins. She crossed her arms over her sagging breasts and spat at me. "You stop looking at me like that. You know too much already. You'll end up in a house of detention, mark my words."

"She didn't see anything, Mom," my sister Beady said, coming to my defense.

"Here, put your arm through this nice fresh slip," Katherine said. "Everything's going to be fine. I'm going to put some makeup on you and a little of my talcum powder so you feel fresh."

"I don't want any paint on my face. I'm no hussy," Mom shouted.

"No, hon, just a drop of pink on your lips. So you look pretty," Katherine insisted.

It was a relief when Pop came back with Frank. Minutes later we heard the dreadful siren of the ambulance as it pulled up, and then the interns in white traipsed through our bedroom to lay hold of our mother. I saw Frank shake his head — no straitjacket would be needed. Mom went peacefully, wearing her good navy dress, her hat, and her white gloves. Pop grabbed a shirt and, dressing en route, followed the procession through the crowd of nosy bodies into the ambulance. My sisters and I watched from the parlor window, and then huddled in the dark and cried.

There was a week of diagnosis and then the verdict. She'd be confined in Brooklyn State Hospital for some time, and did we know she was anemic?

PART THREE

What I noticed first when I returned from school to the now empty railroad flat was an awful stillness and the breakdown of routines.

The ironing board cover got badly burned right through to the wood and the iron's cord ran a short because it was yanked from its socket with too much force once too often. The bottom of the big pot buckled because there was no one to warn us about not immersing it in water till it cooled. Dishes piled up at the side of the sink. Beady and I bickered senselessly over banalities: "That's not my dish; I won't wash it." Katherine tried to keep peace by assuming Mom's role, but the commuting to and from her job in Manhattan six days a week left her exhausted. She went from 118 pounds to 110 within a month.

I don't know who tended to Daddy's needs when Mom went away. At first, he arranged for a part-time social worker to come to clean and cook, but she left before we even learned her name, and we fended for ourselves. Daddy gave a sermon about our "pulling together" and "having a system," ending with a lecture emphasizing self-reliance.

We retreated into our private worlds of self-concern. It was each one for herself as the household crumbled, and Daddy's clarion cry of "Solidarity, daughts" missed its aim. We were not a team. I pined for someone to run to and confide in. I missed the symbol of a mother, as well as the obvious comforts she provided — three square meals a day and the impeccably ironed clothes hanging in my closet. I hadn't a clue about how to wash and sort the laundry. Colors bled. A sweater shrank to infant size. I pulled my sock down into my shoe to hide the hole. I once tried rinsing out a blouse the morning I wanted to wear it, scorching it in places when I tried to iron it dry; it stayed damp on my body most of the day. I had never mastered the technique of ironing. Katherine, like Mom, was a whiz at it, but it was all she could do to look after herself. And because she was going steady, her energies went to keeping the front room in company order. The "Queen Bee," always keen on cleanliness and grooming, fought for her piece of turf, too. She hogged the sink and tub on weekends and used up all the dry towels.

Without Mom there as referee and peacemaker, we were constantly at each other's throats. I suppose we'd turned our grief and fears inward and, feeling abandoned, we lashed out at each other in inarticulate rage. None of us could really understand what had happened to Mom; we had no idea how long she would be gone from us.

I was suspicious of the medical terms they used to describe her condition to us. "Nervous breakdown," "mental disorder" seemed like cover-up language for the blood-chilling words I heard as a child: was my mother "crazy," "nuts," "insane"? And were they substituting "hospital" for "bughouse" or "loony bin"? I tossed at night, trying to dislodge these thoughts from my mind; I slept fitfully, temples damp from sweat and tears. I thought that God had taken away my mother's reason because of me and I felt guilty about how I'd been mean to her. If He would only restore it, I vowed I would return to the Church. I made all kinds of promises and bargains with Him: I would never miss mass; I would obey His commandments; I would never commit another sin in word, thought, or deed. To seal my bargain, I doused myself with holy water and kissed the Blessed Virgin's plaster toe. I went to early mass, fasted for Lent, ashed my forehead, and placed fresh palms over my bed. I knelt at the grotto of Saint Sylvester until my knees were numb. In fact, the number they got, the more convinced I became that God heard my plea.

Finally, my prayers interfered with my schoolwork and my grades began to suffer. Pop, seeing me on my knees at my bedside — for now I was praying for marks as well — said mildly, "That's not going to help with the lesson, Anna. You had better spend time with the nose in the book. Even I," he continued, "infidel that I am, believe the mother's saying, 'God helps those who help themselves.' The poor wretched woman at least had sense to know that."

I was not the only one tossing at night. Beatrice, who was not quite sixteen when Mom took sick, had just come through a grueling adolescence. Her reputation for being troublesome in early childhood reached new heights in puberty. She had always led our mother a merry chase and she, too, felt responsible for Mom's breakdown. Years later she'd tell me, "When Mom went off the deep end, I felt I had pushed her."

My father, too, reproached himself. Just prior to Mother's illness, he had taken a job in a hotel barbershop in Manhattan. It was close to his Yugoslav club, where he spent most of his evenings and Sundays, singing in the chorus, playing the violin, and talking politics. He had long since given up hope of my mother accompanying him there. When her mind snapped, I think he blamed himself for neglecting her and not anticipating the danger signals.

Katherine, too, was riddled with guilt, for although she adored Mom, and her relationship with her was that of a loving daughter, from early childhood on she had ruled the roost. But Katherine swears she didn't usurp her position; Mom just loved being bossed by her.

Katherine had difficulties with my father, too. He grew anxious about her when she started going steady and tightened the reins by setting up stricter house rules. No boyfriend or suitor was admitted past the kitchen door. They were to walk down the hall to the parlor, then wait behind closed doors on the couch while Katherine got ready, and then exit the same way. Dad issued an eleven o'clock curfew. The two inner bedroom doors were kept shut and bolted.

But Katherine was twenty at this time, and the young man, Boris Egorenkov, whom she was entertaining in the clean parlor, was getting restless. He barged through our railroad flat and was determined to grab my sister's hand and lead her out of that rut. Daddy became wary of Boris and angry fights resulted.

When the parlor door leading to the bedrooms got broken (either a hinge came loose or the panel cracked), Daddy suspected it had been forced. He couldn't be convinced that the door always stuck because it would swell up with heat. He said, "Someone was trying to get to Katrin."

To an outsider, the subjects of these fights sound inane. But "rows" is too mild a word to describe such battles as "the door fight" or "the boy-crazy battle," which first began as a joke. "Katrin, why you use this expression 'Oh boy'? What means it? You say, 'Boy, I'm tired,' 'Oh boy, I wish I had this or that,' 'Boy, would I feel good if . . . ,' or 'Boy oh boy.' Always boys on the mind. Son a mum bitch. You are boy-crazy."

The veins in my sister's neck stood out. Tears of indignation tumbled down her cheeks. Her voice trembled, but she managed a defense. "You are wrong, Daddy," she said. "It's an expression. It doesn't mean what you're implying. I'm leaving this house and I'm never . . ." The door slammed behind her.

The fights brought flaming tempers and broken hearts, and when they subsided, the air weighed heavy with accusations, appetites ruined, and meals not eaten. Whether it was that particular fight or one of mine and Beady's, I'd suffer colitis attacks afterward. These attacks were always worse, though, before or after a hospital visit to see Mom.

Beady and I had to go visit Mom twice a week; after school on Wednesday and then again on Sunday. I came to dread the bell that ended every Wednesday's schoolday. I had grown sensitive to strangers' knowing and asking questions about my mother, and I felt conspicuous among my schoolmates because I had to get a special pass signed by both the dean and my homeroom teacher for early dismissal. I hated meeting Beady at the gate and taking the El to the bus that would take us to the hospital.

I recall those bus rides all too clearly. I got used to feeling nauseated, but there were times when I curled up in a paralysis of pain, my face in a cold sweat, waiting for a stomach spasm to leave. We would get off the bus at the maze of buildings that was the hospital. Somewhere in all those annexes and wings, wards and floors, we'd finally locate Mom. She was constantly being shifted around. At first she was among the sedated bed patients, where there were no unusual events. But when she was transferred to another, more active, ward, our spirits sank. We had thought her stay in the hospital would be temporary, but all that moving about convinced us that her recovery would not be quick.

We never knew what to expect when we went to visit her; one week she would be sound and reasonable and the next she would have lost her voice from screaming.

On weekdays there were few visitors, since husbands had to work, and the hospital was relatively quiet. Sundays could be pretty harrowing and holidays were worst of all. Oh God, I'd ask myself, why do I have to spend Christmas day there? Christmas meant that I'd have to go three times a week instead of the regular two. Pathetic decorations were taped to the drab walls. A few strings of tinsel hung on an artificial tree. But even if the decorations had been resplendent, the smells, the aura of those wards would have dampened anyone's holiday spirit. On Easter Sundays we'd bring chocolate eggs because Mom always had a sweet tooth. One year I brought her a palm and a rosary and I remember the whole hospital stinking with the sickly sweet smell of hyacinths, their clay pots covered with garish pink or green foil.

Since Mom was a ward patient our visits were seldom private. Other patients stood around and there were occasional flare-ups. There was a woman, Marie, about thirty-five, who wore anklets and butterfly barrettes in her hair. During one of our visits, she ran to my mother's bed, curt-sied, and picked up her dress to show us her bloomers. Her knees were fat with faces in them. When she touched my hair and said, "Pretty," I was too frightened to respond and Mom screamed, "Get away from my people, Marie! You've got your own family. You're just here to get my jelly beans." Marie spat at her, which sent the nurses scurrying over. "Now, Marie, stop bothering Stella," one of them said. "I'm going to have to send your mother home if you don't behave."

Marie's mother came pleading up to her. She looked ancient and spoke with a heavy accent. "Be good, sweetheart. Be nice, Marie." Things quieted down, we all took our seats again, and then, like a gust of wind, Marie flew up and struck someone standing next to her. It happened so fast that nobody saw it coming. Suddenly, a bevy of nurses and interns were grabbing and dragging her away and her screams of protest unnerved everyone. Mom looked away from her and then, shivering with indignation, said, "That's the kind of place you send me to, John. These are the kind of people I have to contend with. If I was ever sane, they'd drive me crazy."

In the elevator with other departing visitors, we would hear the awful hysterical cries of those left behind. We all pretended not to notice by fixing our attention on the blinking floor numbers as we descended to the lobby. We hurried down the front walk to the waiting buses. Fists shook at us from the barred windows above, arms reached out, accusations screamed after us, "You're all against me!" "I don't belong here!" "You want my money, you fucking shit ass.... Come back, pleeeese!"

In the early part of her hospitalization, when Mom had perfectly rational periods, she would come home on trial visits. She didn't try to reestablish her role as homemaker, though. It seemed strange, if not unnatural, to have her back, sitting on the couch with my father cuddling her. I felt awkward and nervous and couldn't talk or laugh the way I usually did. I sensed my father's need for her, and when I would look at him he'd blush, knowing I knew.

One weekend she arrived wearing her blue crepe traveling dress, which Katherine pressed and spruced up by adding organdy ruffles. Katherine had married Boris by then, and that night we all went to dinner at her new in-laws' to celebrate. Daddy smiled at everyone and toasted the Egorenkovs in Russian while Mom sat rigid in a high-backed chair. I don't think she ate, because the food was foreign to her, and I know she didn't even sip the wine. As Daddy got a little tipsy and tried to keep things going, Katherine grew quiet and tense. It wasn't until Boris's sisters and his brother came that the tension in the room relaxed. It became festive, and even Mom seemed to enjoy herself.

But the trial visit ended abruptly and when Mom had to return to the hospital, she was angry and hurt. Her accusations were pitiable, her pleas justified. And Daddy had no answer for her. What could he say? She said she didn't want to go back to that place and live behind bars. "What crime have I committed? What do they mean by saying I was bad, Daddy? I'm not a child." She seemed never to call my father John anymore.

At any time, a look, a sound would set off one of her lapses into sly and irrational behavior. When she was home, Daddy had to be on constant watch; she was never to be left alone. After this vigilance, it was a sad relief for all of us when she went back.

Daddy grew morose and harder to live with when Katherine married and moved out. I didn't know she was gone until one day I noticed Beatrice's clothes hanging in her closet. Kay's leaving meant I would inherit a twin bed and peace at last from the parlor couch and all the sounds of Liberty Avenue. But not even having my own new bed could make up for the letdown I felt.

We still saw Katherine from time to time, and she continued in her role as surrogate mother. She arranged for my graduation gown to be made by her mother-in-law, who selected a preteen pattern for an ankle-length white taffeta dress. Daddy bought me a new brown three-quarter-length coat, which was too sporty for a corsage and too straight to accommodate my bustle. But I didn't mind, having grown practical with age; I wasn't really concerned with fashion anyway. I had the white dress I'd been longing for ever since my nonconfirmation days. Although I was grateful to Mrs. Egorenkov for making it, I couldn't help wondering what my own mother would have selected for me.

After graduation, I left Junior High School 171 with no melancholy backward glances, for my time there had been a disaster. Until junior high I had coped with being small for my age and other difficulties by excelling academically. My goal was to be the smartest kid in the class and I usually succeeded. Because of my grades, I was enrolled in a junior high program called Rapid Advance, which presumably was designed to get the best students out of school more quickly by giving them a heavier work load.

Unfortunately, I was not up to the program, in part because I was emotionally devastated by Mom's breakdown, which had occurred at the same time. My mind was full of jumbled lessons. Dates and data, formulas and facts, all went in one ear and instead of going out the other, they collided somewhere in the middle of my head. I was totally confused and in no way ready to advance rapidly to high school. I would have completely despaired in junior high had it not been for Miss Edwards, the English teacher. I was her prize student. She headed the dramatics club, of which I may have been the only member. At least, I don't recall having any competition at all. She kept me busy doing monologues and presented me weekly in the assembly. I headed the speech class and I was selected as spokesman and orator for school politicians. Although I never ran for any office myself because my grades weren't good enough, I performed as a "booster" for other candidates. My confidence returned and I became enterprising, and graduated from junior high with some dignity.

I saw Franklin K. Lane High School, where I was headed, for the first time when Beady, who was a student there, sang in the chorus of *The Pirates of Penzance*. The assembly hall completely overwhelmed me: the auditorium, which held 1,500 people, was sharply raked, and a grand piano sat at one side of the raised stage. The red velvet curtain with gold fringe was caught back in a graceful swag. Footlights exposed the enormous depth of the stage.

Beady had been at Lane for two years when I came along. If she said it once, she said it a thousand times: "I'm a Laneite — that's why I'm entitled to wear the school sweater."

She talked Daddy into buying her white boots, copied from those of Sonja Henie, the Olympic skating star. They were the popular footgear of the day and looked very chic with her white sweater with the big blue L on it. When Aunt Anne visited New York for the World's Fair, Lane was on her list of "Sights to See." Beady, of course, clad in her sweater and boots, gave the guided tour; I tagged behind. Aunt Anne, the soul of diplomacy, understood Beady's possessive pride and gently included me in her comments: "You girls are lucky to be enrolled here. It's a beautiful school!" she said. Beady begrudgingly allowed that it might be large enough for both of us.

Lane High School was indeed huge: not trick-of-the-memory huge, not a young girl's idea of huge, but huge by anybody's standards. It was described as one of the largest academic buildings in the world when it opened in 1937. The red brick colonial-style building with white Doric columns covered one square block of Jamaica Avenue next to a cemetery. A grandstand and a ball park adjoined the school and there were softball fields and tennis courts on the cemetery side.

In this setting, real-world concerns intruded on our fumbling progress to adulthood. By my senior year boys were being drafted immediately after graduation and special societies were formed for Laneites overseas. Honor rolls were printed and girls married soldiers even before graduating. There was talk of a girl being pregnant and having to leave school before the prom, and there was a case of miscegenation involving a girl in my Latin class and a Negro basketball star that shocked the school.

Because I squeaked through Rapid Advance, I entered Lane as a sophomore, although I felt neither physically nor mentally equal to my peers. I was still referred to as "the little red-headed girl" or "shorty" and treated as a lowly freshman. There was no Miss Edwards to run to anymore. When I joined Miss Miller's dramatic club, I had quite a lot of competition for the limelight. I was no longer the school actress, the Big Cheese; in fact, I was small potatoes now.

I was overwhelmed by Lane and I responded by withdrawing and becoming inhibited. Suddenly, boys terrified me. I stared at them from safe distances and couldn't meet their gazes. I envied and marveled at the courage of girls who could casually hold hands with boys and keep in step with them.

I fell passionately in love with a boy I never spoke a word to. I called him Arnie because his surname was Arnold and I never knew his first name. I first spotted him in the cafeteria, sitting at a table in the sunlight. The mesh guard on the window laid a pattern on his white sweater. On the back of his head sat a white cap with a tiny brim that folded down in front. His pants were rolled to the ankle, he wore white sweat socks and sneakers — summer and winter, as I discovered. I thought I was dreaming when he joined my biology class. The teacher welcomed him and said, "Mr. Arnold, will you please remove your cap?" Arnie reluctantly pulled his cap off and his cowlick popped up.

Even though he was in my class, I never heard him speak. About the only sign of life he demonstrated was to rearrange his legs at the teacher's insistence; they were blocking the aisle. He always sat waiting, hat in hand, for the bell to ring, and when it sounded, he was out the door before the second clang. Hot on his trail, I raced after him through the hall and watched him skid to a stop at Room 215. Out came the twins, two of the most popular girls in school. Tall and willowy, they wore dangling in their long brown hair pink satin ribbons that matched their sweaters and knee socks. Arnie, a lovesick puppy, shuffled into step with them, cocking his hat at different angles, animated and laughing. I followed behind, but Arnie never saw me. After seeing the twins, I raced to the 5 and 10 for pink ribbons and socks, but even so attired, I could never catch his eye. It was months before I gave up the futile pursuit.

Fortunately, I soon became fast friends with Louise, who more than any single person helped me navigate the treacherous emotional waters of adolescence. I first saw her in French I, wearing a bright red sweater with matching bows bobby-pinned over each ear. She looked like a cross between Anna May Wong and Claudette Colbert. Her jet-black hair was a pleasing contrast to her pale skin and she had huge brown eyes as trusting as a puppy's. She knew the effect of rolling those eyes, for I spotted a devilish streak in Louise from the start. That first day in class, she established herself as class clown by bandying wits with Madame Gross, our French teacher. Madame was a refugee from Germany with a heavy and guttural accent. When she announced our first French *lezzon*, self-conscious titters arose across the room. She attempted to put us at our ease by speaking slowly and deliberately. "Lizzen," she said, "I am going to tell you my name. I will say, in French: 'My name is Mrs. Gross' and then I will ask you yours. So — *alors, je m'appelle Madame Gross.* Now, lizzen: *comment vous appellez-vous, mademoiselle?*"

Louise volunteered and, mimicking the French-German accent to perfection, said: *"Je m'abell Mademoiselle Grozzz."*

The class shrieked. But Madame Gross knew how to handle little girls with tendencies to show off: "Ah," she responded, lifting her brows in mock surprise, "we have the same name, I see; I am very pleased to find I have such a pretty relative." Louise's eyes melted like chocolate in the sun. She brought her hands to her face and giggled an apology.

We met again the following term in the dramatic society and were cast in the same play. She played the part of my best friend. We carried the relationship off stage and became inseparable. Our friendship was steadfast, lasting throughout high school and into adulthood.

Louise was different from most of the girls at Lane, who came from ultraconservative families and lived in two-family brownstone houses. They all had little watches and kept their nails short — they took typing and shorthand — and wore colorless nail polish. Louise, like me, took a general academic course. Though she looked demure in repose, she had a fiery Latin temperament. We lived at least two El stops from each other, but we managed to be together constantly. She had a grasp of life well beyond her years and she exercised a strong influence on me.

I imitated everything she did. From Louise I learned that my knee socks had to match my shetland sweater and that the length of the sweater was crucial — it had to come down over the hips so only six inches of pleated skirt showed. The sleeves were then pushed up midarm. I wore my hair shoulder-length in a pageboy and cut my bangs like hers. To complete the look, I had a single strand of pearls hanging almost to my knees. I bought a trench coat like hers and wrote on it with blue ink. I wrote on my saddle shoes, too — we were walking graffitti. She taught me the useful trick of copying French verb conjugations and Latin declensions on my shoes before a test. If it rained, the ink smeared and I was outfoxed — the ablative and the subjunctive blurred into each other.

I marveled at Louise's sophisticated air. She could make a perfect bow on her lips without using a mirror. Though I never quite achieved that, I kept borrowing her purple lipstick and trying. She inhaled cigarettes, allowing

the smoke to filter through her nose. I never could do that,
either. But I did achieve her walk, which is best described as
the saddle-shoe walk of the forties — I bounced on the balls
of my feet, on those smooth bubblegum-pink rubber soles. I
went swinging along, as if to the strains of Tommy Dorsey's
orchestra, and the pleats in my skirt swayed from side to
side. Almost all the girls in high school walked that way,
but Louise had her own special version, and mine was
based on hers.

Louise's influence on me extended beyond outward
appearances and modish behavior, however. Our talks on
every subject imaginable are among my richest and most
lasting memories. There was a serious side to Louise, which
she showed only to intimates. I could talk to her about my
mother because she understood my terror of revealing my
mother's illness, my sense of family disgrace, and she was
careful to let me know she understood. She told me about
her family life. Her oldest sister, Marion, was an invalid and
that caused tensions and problems for Louise. Her mother
was naturally overprotective of the oldest girl, an absolute
beauty whom Louise closely resembled, and she discour-
aged boys from calling until Marion found someone too.
But Louise couldn't wait. Unlike me, she was not content to
eye boys from a distance and had by the time I met her
developed a fair amount of social savvy. Under her coaching, I became eager for a more realistic social life, too.

Before I met Louise, I was on the outside looking in. I
passed the Blue Corner, an ice cream parlor on Jamaica
Avenue, and longed to go in and hang out with the crowd,
but I was too scared and meek to attempt it until Louise
looped her arm through mine and led me in. In no time we
left the counter stools and headed for a front booth next to
the jukebox, where the seniors sat. Once my foot was in the

door, I became an habitué, calling it the "B.C." and chatting with the owners on a first-name basis. But it was really Louise who took all the steps first. She joined the crowd and went dancing at the Y every Friday and Saturday night. Then she taught me to jitterbug, pulling me to my feet and pushing me into action, preparing me to join her at the Y dances.

What a thrill it was to dance in the blue silk dress with accordion pleats Katherine had given me. I never dreamed I'd see the day when I'd be able to go out on the floor in the darkened hall and dip and twirl and spin. I wasn't a particularly good dancer, but I was eager and energetic. I could dance well with boys I trusted and cared about, and I danced especially well with Richy. He knew how to hold a girl and maneuver, no matter how crowded the floor. He was aggressive without being boorish. Even though he was a tough kid from a rough section of east New York, he held doors open, walked on the outside, and took my arm when we crossed streets. After our first kiss, which caused an explosion of unbounded love in me, he asked me to go steady. I assented, of course, and could hardly wait to tell Louise, since she had been my real instructor in sex and courtship.

Daddy had made a halfhearted effort to broach the subject of boys and my physical changes by asking veiled questions. "Have you had monthly sickness?" "Ask Katherine to explain things." I could only guess at what those "things" implied. Even though I was not considering sexual activity in high school, I wanted to know what was in store for me in the future. I wanted to know about life because I had no intention of trapping a man by getting caught.

Louise clued me in to the "facts of life." I recall vividly how she eased my curiosity and confusion. She made me aware that girls liked sex as much as men did and, furthermore, she said, "It's fun. But unless you're willing to go all the way, Anna Jane, you must not excite the fellas because it's unfair to be a tease." She called things by their rightful names: a penis was a penis and a vagina a vagina. She reproved me if I cloaked my language. "Anna Jane," she said, "if you ever think of having intercourse, you must make sure you find out if they have contraceptives. Otherwise, they should withdraw. Now in passionate moments you may forget, so make sure before it comes to that that you discuss it."

"Well, how, though?" I sputtered. "I can't just come out and say those things."

"Yes you can. You have to. If you find yourself getting carried away, make sure you say, 'I don't want to get pregnant. Do you have protection?' Anna Jane, you must."

I was pleased to be able to repay Louise by being her confidant and consoler when her romance with her boyfriend, Buddy, broke up. I had just returned from a visit to my mother, and Louise was standing on our doorstep. Her mascara had run and streaked her heart-shaped face. My father pretended not to notice. She and I raced up the flights of stairs and settled in the parlor. I quietly closed the door and she broke into heartrending sobs. She held out her sun-tanned finger, where there was a white band instead of Buddy's ring. I learned from disjointed sentences that they had broken up.

"Oh, Anna Jane, I don't know what I'll do without him. I never let any fellow go as far and he's the only guy I'll ever love.

"He asked Gladys Wertheimer to go to the Y dance next Saturday. I can't go. I can't see him with her or I'll drop dead! So please go and tell me everything. Don't, for

God's sake, tell Richy anything. I know you think because you go steady you should tell him everything, but I swear to God, he'll only make matters worse." Within a few weeks Louise and Buddy got together while jitterbugging to "That Old Black Magic," and we were a foursome again.

I made her promise she'd come with Buddy when Richy came to meet my father. Oh, how I dreaded that encounter.

Richy wasn't handsome by conventional standards: he wasn't the Smiling Jack of the comic strip type, jawed with a crewcut. He was a "sharpie" in a zoot suit with crooked teeth. He wore his hair in a Sinatra-like pompadour, which broke into a thousand ringlets when he danced. At seventeen he had laugh lines around his eyes and mouth. I was attracted to the sad, forlorn look which crept into his eyes when he was off guard. If he caught me noticing it, he switched moods, got silly, and began to strut. I was afraid to have Daddy meet him, because I knew he wouldn't measure up. Daddy wouldn't see what I saw. He'd be thrown by the zoot suit, the long key chain, the porkpie hat sitting on Richy's head like a pan. He'd wonder about those pegged pants and padded shoulders. The clothes and the devil-may-care attitude would be unfavorable, but Richy's real handicap, as far as my father was concerned, would be his lack of "awareness." He had no social conscience and he wasn't out to right the world's wrongs. In fact, that forlorn look I saw in his eyes was his acknowledgment of life's futility, which he couldn't begin to articulate. It was a look of endurance and forbearance. My father looked for men of defiance; he wanted rebels for his daughters.

Louise understood my anxiety, and she and Buddy were at my house when Richy called to pick me up for a date. My father let him in and after I introduced him, he looked him up and down, placed his hands on his hips and said, "Sit down, young man. Let's have little talk. First, what are your political views? What do you know of world events and what are your intentions?"

"Daddy, please," I moaned. "God almighty!"

"God has nothing to do with it and I must be both father and mother now, so I must know these things. I supposed to interview and guide so these young men know what story is. My girls can't boil the water. They have no sense of what means housekeeping but they know what is expected of them as human beings. They are beginning to have political awareness."

"Well, gee, Mr. Jackson," Richy said. He cleared his throat, smiled self-consciously, and then added, "That's solid!" He stood there, twirling his hat.

Daddy sighed deeply and gave strict instructions. "I expect my daughter to be in house by ten-thirty, not one minute past." The handshake was desultory.

Not long afterward, Richy and I parted ways. While we were dancing at the pool one summer night, he told me he wanted to break up. I ran all the way home, crying, with Louise in pursuit. Pain of rejection racked my body; thoughts of suicide and revenge raced through my head.

"Now listen," Louise said, when my sobs subsided. "I know Richy is crazy about you. He even told Buddy; but he needs a girl he can go all the way with. He respects you and I know he tried to get fresh with you at Adeline's party but that was because he was drunk. He felt bad, I'm sure. Your best bet is to pretend you don't care. That's how I got Buddy back. Go out with another fellow and he'll come crawling on hands and knees. Unless it's his mother. If she wants him to go with an Italian girl, then, Anna Jane, believe me, it won't work out. Italian mothers are very strong-willed where their sons are concerned."

I took Louise's advice and went to the Y dance with another fellow, but the pain lingered. When Richy arrived with another girl on his arm, Louise rushed to my side. I couldn't hear "Green Eyes" without crying. We never got back together again.

Gradually I underwent a personality change. I read more and became critical of my friends. I plunged whole-heartedly into acting and joined an adult drama class held in the evenings. The teacher introduced me to the name Stanislavski. I no longer wanted to hang out with "my crowd"; the Y dances and frivolous sixteen-year-olds lazing on Rockaway Beach held little attraction for me anymore.

At sixteen, I left the Catholic Church again and became a socialist. I got into political discussions and argued with Louise. "But Anna Jane," she'd say, "for Italy, Mussolini is very good. My parents remember the country before he came to power and unified the people. You can't lump Mussolini with Hitler, because another nation is involved."

I argued heatedly about the evils of fascism throughout the world. "Don't you understand?" I screeched, "that the fascists only care about the rich and the few? What about the people? What about the poor who have to earn their bread by the sweat of their brows?" The clichés came at rapid fire.

"Anna Jane, that's communism you're talking about. I'm talking about social improvements like roads and housing, not communism, where they kill nuns and priests!" Arguing in circles, I'd speak for the sake of hearing myself.

I quoted the Sermon on the Mount along with catch phrases I had picked up from my father. When I started showing off too much, Louise would bring me down to earth by asking, "How's your mother, Anna Jane?" shifting from high-minded talk to compassionate concern in the bat of an eye. When I'd get critical of my father and complain about his being strict or unreasonable, she would gently remind me of his circumstances. "You know, Anna Jane, it's very hard on your Dad not having your mother around and raising you two growing girls. You really shouldn't get too mad at him when he drinks; he's a very unusual man." Louise and I had our differences, but we remained close friends.

In my senior year, I fell in love with a boy on the backstage crew. No more devil-may-care zoot-suiters for me. My new boyfriend, Dave, played basketball, was extremely handsome and intelligent. He painted well and with my coaching began to read. Whitman became his God and *Leaves of Grass* his Bible.

Our stormy romance lasted for almost three years. We would quarrel about the silliest things and I remember breaking up, crying, vowing never to see him again, never to fall in love again. Then, soon afterward we'd make up and be two against the world once more. I think of him as my first real love because our relationship went beyond youthful passions. We became engaged when he went into basic training.

When I graduated from high school in the winter of 1943, I applied for a nine-to-five job. Wearing a hand-me-down suit, new high-crowned hat with a feather, spectator pumps, and Bea's old garter belt to hold up my sheer stockings, I passed for at least eighteen. I landed an office job as "tracer" for an insurance company on Wall Street.

What a lovely sense of adventure to travel during rush hour, buy a newspaper and race up the El steps to catch my train! I felt a part of the hustle and bustle and liked seeing early-morning faces and smelling coffee breath and shaving cream. There were still a few civilian men to exchange glances with and daydream about.

Looking into my own windows as the El rushed by and seeing into other people's was an odd and new sensation. Glimpsing nudity and catching people unaware, I realized why Mom had kept yelling about "closing that window" or "drawing that blind so people can't see in."

I liked being with other passengers. I felt secure in the knowledge that I had someplace to go, and earning money made me feel proud and important. At first, I buried my face in the newspaper like the other commuters, but when the ink soiled my white gloves, I took to carrying novels instead. Katherine's books passed from Beady on to me. I remember reading *Native Son* and getting so involved that I rode past my stop. One morning I looked up and caught a man in "civvies" craning his neck to read the title of my book. I could tell in a glance that he disapproved, but I could not say whether it was a moral or political judgment, since the book was considered leftist and had some sexy passages. At any rate, I gave up reading on the train after that. I found it disconcerting that the lights flickered and the cars swayed from side to side. The motion, noise, and abrupt plunge underground made reading uncomfortable. I people-watched instead.

I noticed that the same group of passengers boarded the train by the same doors at the same times each morning and that they took the same seats or stood in the same relative positions. The woman wearing the brown velour hat always sat opposite me and tugged at her skirt, greatly concerned about keeping her knees together. I was one of the herd watching the herd and soon experienced what they experienced — that sense of superiority over passengers who boarded the train after me and didn't get a seat. Those with window seats felt an even greater sense of superiority; they didn't have to crane their necks to check the station signs. I soon learned to adopt subway attitudes: your subway face remained impersonal; you never smiled or acknowledged the person sitting opposite or next to you. This game of pretending "not to see, not to be, not to notice anything" intrigued me.

It was a triumph of self-control for me not to break into laughter at times. One morning the lady across the aisle started an argument with a stout lady, who squeezed into a seat next to her. A skinny man left the seat and when the stout lady settled in, there was a grunt of indignation because she sat on the flap of the other woman's coat. The entire row of people was involved in spatial repositioning and irritation at the newcomer traveled like an electric shock from body to body. The stout woman defended her position by saying, "I paid my nickel fare, so don't act like you own the train, because you don't own the train."

Life at the insurance office soon lost its exotic allure. I began to get bored with Wall Street. Being office staff was like being back in school. A supervisor sat on a platform so she could oversee her staff of girls. All the personnel were women except two cranky old men, the company lawyers, who sat in cubicles behind frosted panels. When I entered their cubicles, they never even looked up. It was hard to distinguish one from the other and I was constantly getting the cases and numbers they gave me mixed up.

The girl who sat beside me was engaged to a sailor

who was off in the Pacific. She wrote him letters on the sly during the day. Except for the lipstick kisses she planted on the flaps of the envelopes, there wasn't a lick of color about her. Her clothes were file-cabinet grey. There were no knickknacks or signs of life anywhere about her desk or her person. For that matter, there was no life in any part of that office. A peep through the slats of blinds to the next office building reflected the same drab scene.

I tried to brighten things up a bit by wearing my saddle shoes to work and bouncing about in bright colored skirts and sweaters. When I put out a picture of my G.I. boyfriend, my colorless neighbor said he looked "cute" and then showed me the wallet photo of her sailor. The picture was cracked and the corners torn off from so much handling.

When I hurried with my work so that I'd have more time to myself to read, I found I was simply given more work. In my boredom, I tried to stir things up a bit by chirping good morning to the grouchy men and trying to interest the grey girl in reading *Native Son*. I failed on these fronts and began to sense a coldness. I was soon clued in to the do's and don'ts of office workers: You don't show up the other girls by doing your job faster, and you don't read books like mine at the office. Also, it would be better if I curbed my enthusiasm. That meant no big good mornings and no humming, whistling, or giggling at my desk.

I owed these insights to an Irish girl in her late twenties who was assistant to the supervisor. She stopped by my desk one afternoon and closed a book I was reading. "Let's go to the washroom and have a cig." I tagged in after her and she said, jabbing her pinky into her lipstick tube, "I know you get your work done faster than the others but it's not because you're smarter. It's because you don't know how to stall." She winked at me as she wiped the stain off her little finger. "There are no medals here for fastest tracer and you're not in a personality contest either, so take it easy and simmer down. You'll last longer." Then she blew excess powder from her puff, pressed it to the crease in her nose and held the compact away from her body as she clicked it shut.

When the grey girl asked me about my boyfriend, later that afternoon, I told her he was an artist and a poet. She grew quiet and her brows furrowed. I knew I had scared her off again when she said, "The army will help him a lot and if you plan to get married, he'll definitely straighten up and fly right." There was really no more to be said. I put Dave's picture in my purse and tried to look busy.

The only escape from tedium in that office was to open the folders and read the cases. It was a contact with humanity and I grew curious to know what I was getting paid for. The grey girl also entertained herself in this way. One afternoon just before five she got the giggles and ran to the water cooler to cure her hiccoughs. She had slipped an open folder under my nose and pointed to a case she wanted me to read. It was an accident report written by a claimant for workmen's compensation. It read: "I went to the men's room to relieve myself on Friday March 14, at 4:30 and the toilet flushed scalding water, causing me to burn my parts." It was so bizarre that I found myself laughing hysterically. The whole office of workers looked my way. My mascara burned my eyes and I ran blindly toward the washroom. The following morning I gave two weeks' notice.

After Easter I applied for a job as an elevator operator in the Chrysler Building, filling in for an absentee soldier. It paid thirty-five dollars a week, which was more money than I had ever made, so I was determined to get the job, though

I had to lie about my age and my religion. (I'd been warned that unless I was eighteen and Protestant I'd automatically be eliminated.) The other important requirement was appearance, for which Katherine gave me careful priming. "They are very particular. You have to look good in the uniform, so wear something trim and neat. Wear stockings —no streaky leg makeup with a line drawn in eyebrow pencil up the back will do. And your shoes should have a sensible heel. Boy, if you can land this job, kiddo, it will be a coup."

I polished my cuban-heeled shoes and washed my white cotton gloves as Katherine pressed the pleats in my dress. After a fitful sleep in aluminum curlers, I went to my interview and I was hired. I pranced up East Forty-second Street, went to the Commodore Hotel to phone Katherine, stopped in the automat and had a fishcake and baked beans. I started work that afternoon, riding up and down with a girl who showed me the ropes. Once I got the hang of leveling the car I was on my own.

There was excitement the first few days; a sense of power in driving my car up and down, eliminating passenger after passenger. The initial difficulties waned with experience, and I learned to fence off my car by holding out an arm: "Sorry. That's capacity." The monotony of the job was relieved in the mornings, lunch hours, and evenings when there were crowds. Janice, the other operator, tuned me in on the execs who remained at Texaco despite the war. She knew the draft dodgers and warned me about horny guys, wolves, and the "nice" messenger kids. "Look," she said, "the first week you're here the guys are gonna wait for your car 'cause you're new. You just have to watch out for the ones who start sidling up. And there are a couple who can't keep their hands to themselves, so try not to get them alone in the car."

I soon got to know which office girls were set up in Greenwich Village apartments by married men with kids growing up in Greenwich, Connecticut. This job made me feel deceitful. Obviously, we'd been hired to keep up the morale of these guys at home and I didn't mind riding up and down with the young men my age who were about to be drafted, but some of the older married men were annoying. I just lasted the summer before I found a part-time job as a salesgirl in a chocolate shop on West Forty-second Street. Geographically at least, it brought me closer to Broadway.

The chocolate shop marked a period of transition in my life. It was run by German refugees who let me dress as I liked and read what I pleased. They encouraged me in my aspirations to the stage; their support stimulated my initiative.

On my lunch hours I'd seek out information from out-of-work actors who hung out at the Walgreen's lunch counter on Forty-fourth Street. While lunching there I learned of drama classes at the New School, and I decided to go downtown and apply.

I found sand from Rockaway Beach in my trench coat pocket as I fished out the nickel fare for that first ride, a reminder of my beach days at Rockaway, where my G.I. boyfriend and I lay in the sun holding hands and necking into the evening. We'd return home sandy and salty, giddy with sunburn's hot and cold chills. While he was in basic training, our letters had ranged from admissions of physical hunger and desire and proclamations of everlasting need to philosophical essays on poetry, art, and truth. He was suspicious of my acting, calling it "a phony profession," which made me feel self-conscious about admitting my deep-seated aspirations for an acting career. Again, it was my old fear of ridicule, my fear that he'd challenge me with "What makes her think she can be an actress? Boy, she must think she's hot stuff." I was never able to verbalize my need for the theatre to anyone. I didn't think I was "hot stuff," but I did have personality, persistence, and passion. I cared about people. I cared about life I wanted to help right the world's wrongs. I wanted everyone to understand me and I wanted to understand everyone else. What other requirement did a human being need to be an actress?

My fiancé and I fought and separated. I wrote a good-bye letter. We never renewed our romance once the war ended.

A new chapter opened for me when I arrived in Greenwich Village and searched out the New School. An actor acquaintance had written Herbert Berghof's name on a Walgreen's napkin for me, saying he thought I should study acting with him. I went in search of my teacher. I appeared before Berghof wearing bobby socks and saddle shoes, carrying Joyce's *Ulysses* under my arm. A mild man with a Viennese accent peered at me with his shiny sea-green eyes from behind hornrimmed glasses. His hair formed a wreath around his balding head. Herbert was then and still is flirtatious, curious, and shy. He stood, shifting his weight from one leg to another, one knee boyishly bent. He scratched the middle of his back while he talked to me, giving the impression of an awkward adolescent in a mature body. I liked him immediately. He seemed surprised when I told him I wanted to study the Stanislavski Method. In spite of his first impression of me as a brash American bobby-soxer, he invited me to join his sessions.

Each Thursday evening, I traveled to class in the Village. Eagerness mounted each time the subway train crawled into the West Fourth Street station. I walked up Sixth Avenue with a spring in my step, turning into Twelfth Street and gazing into ground-floor parlor windows at walls of books. I always responded to the atmosphere of the Village; the very air smelled different. No ticker-tape, inky-typewriter smells here, no steel-cabinet grey. The bohemian atmosphere excited me with a sense of belonging. I loved it. Herbert Berghof's classes whetted my appetite and increased my craving to act, though I still thought of the theatre as an escape from reality. Berghof would help me discover how the two are inextricably entwined.

Herbert was directing one of our class projects and offered me a part I found I couldn't handle. I read the stage directions with a sinking heart — my character had to "break down and cry." I grew tense with anxiety, and at the end of the session I went to him and said, "Mr. Berghof, I'm afraid I can't play this part."

He opened his eyes in surprise, and, frowning, asked, "Oh? I don't understand. Why not, Annie?"

"Because," I answered, "I'm a comedienne."

"Ya?" he said, leaving the moment in suspension, and seeking further explanation he asked, "What do you mean by that?"

"I mean I don't play crying parts," I answered.

"Well, you know what? We'll cross out stage directions." After a significant pause he added, "You know,

Annie, as in real life, nobody ever plans to cry." He'd opened the door a crack for me.

Herbert was going to teach at the Neighborhood Playhouse that fall and he suggested that I apply for a scholarship to study acting full-time. He paved the way for my interviews with Sandy Meisner, the renowned acting teacher, who had a reputation for being tough and aloof. After what seemed to me a rather cursory interview, I got up to leave. My hand on the doorknob shook so much that he had to turn it for me, and with a gentle shove, he sent me on my way. Much to my surprise, I was granted a full scholarship.

I commuted each weekday from Valley Stream, Long Island, where I lived with Katherine and her husband, Boris. On weekends I baby-sat for my niece, Judith, to earn some pin money, food, and board. Thus subsidized, I could easily concentrate on my studies. At nine months, Judy was audience to all of Shakespeare's sonnets, a lot of Sheridan, as well as all my speech exercises.

Learning to speak standard English was the hardest task for me, and probably for most young actors, because I had to put up with a lot of ridicule from everyday people. This bothered me until I heard a story about the actress Stella Adler, who was shopping and clipped her speech when she spoke to a salesgirl. Her A's were naturally broadening when a clerk asked, "Are you English?" to which Stella replied, "No, just affected." That gave me heart and determination to press on. If I wanted to play a variety of parts and avoid being typed, I'd have to standardize my speech. With that aim in mind, I determinedly proceeded.

I enjoyed the structure of classes at the Neighborhood

Playhouse, especially Martha Graham's modern dance class. When we weren't rehearsing and improvising, she had us pony-trotting around and contracting and contorting our bodies. I could have spent every hour of every day in these classes, they were so inspiring. I responded especially to the eloquence of her talks, not to mention her passion. "There is a vitality, a life force and energy, a quickening, which is translated through you into action, and because there is only one of you in all time, this expression is unique. And if you block it, it will never exist through any other medium and will be lost. The world will not have it." The world was going to have me.

A class with her inspired me to acts of folly. I'd leave the train in Valley Stream, run barefoot past the commuters across Sunrise Highway and prance on the grass. I was the talk of Valley Stream because I practiced leaping over the lawns; this made Judy laugh and clap in her playpen, and the neighbors gawk in disbelief.

This year was a very happy time for me. I was part of a family. I loved sharing my sister's baby and pretended she was mine when I took her walking in the little park near the train station. My sister's suburban house was close to an airfield, and at night when I was left alone, I pretended that the planes flying overhead were bombers. As I imagined the air raid sirens, I would run with Judy in my arms from room to room, a babushka on my head, and I'd duck under the bed with her. Acting was becoming more and more part of my everyday life.

My father was not pleased when I left home to live with Katherine, but he was preoccupied with my mother's illness and spent time working and living at the hospital, cutting patients' hair or gardening on the grounds and keeping an eye on Mom's condition. Beady was left alone in Brooklyn.

On weekends he returned and escorted both of us to his Yugoslav club. There he could speak Croatian, sing in the chorus, drown his sorrows in schnapps, and dance the polka. We would watch Daddy on the dance floor, his jacket off, his shirtsleeves rolled up, his partner held at arm's length. He bent his body in the position of a squat, more like the preparation for a wrestling match than a dance. He bounced up and down in place, and then tore into a wild whiz of the polka in two-four time. I saw the blurred face of Mrs. Solchek, his partner, her eyeglasses bobbing, her face flushed scarlet as he pushed and shoved her around the dance floor. Beady and I stood helplessly by and we noticed the relief on Mrs. Solchek's face as he all but threw her back to our corner. When the band struck up the waltz, Pop sat it out; it was just too sentimental for him, or maybe he was thinking of Mom. Was there ever a time, I wondered, when they danced together?

To his delight, Beady met and fell in love with a young man there. I was polka-ing with Pop and I saw Beady and my future brother-in-law eyeing each other from the sidelines. Emil was born in Trieste but raised in the Bay Ridge section of Brooklyn. He was interested in building and sailing boats, owned an accordion, and was a devotee of classical music. When he married my sister and went off to the navy, he left both Beatrice and his accordion in my father's safekeeping.

But my social life didn't center around the Yugoslav club. I got involved with a lot of older and more experienced students at the Playhouse. They took me to concerts and dance recitals, and we sneaked into plays together, catching the second act of everything on Broadway. The only hit I managed to see in its entirety was *The Glass Menagerie*, starring Laurette Taylor, and her performance sent me into a transport of awed admiration. I saw her play at least four times after that, and could never see the wheels working. I had the neophyte's arrogance to criticize and find fault with almost all other performances except Laurette's.

These extracurricular activities kept me in town later and later, and often I would barely catch the late train back to Valley Stream, shirking my part of the bargain with Katherine to help at the dinner hour and babysit. Quarrels ensued. One evening Boris tore into me for being late, inconsiderate, and selfish. Standing above him on the staircase, I couldn't control the impulse to stage the scene. As he was pressing me for answers as to why the hell I was so irresponsible, I took a deep diaphragmatic breath, and in a voice neighbors heard for miles around, I said, "Don't ask me bourgeois questions! You of all people, Boris, because I am an artist." That took the wind out of him. His astonished laughter sent me racing upstairs. Shaking with rage, I slammed the bathroom door behind me. I saw my face in the mirror and noted a look of disappointment. Shouldn't I have gotten a round of applause when I exited?

But when life returned to normal, in the quiet hours of rational thinking, I knew I had to move on. So I had to make a momentous decision to try and live on my own as soon as I could find a job that would pay the rent.

A publicity release for the John Golden talent auditions appeared in my mailbox at school. "Everybody gets a chance to be heard," the letter promised. Mr. Kaufman, Golden's stage manager, whose brainchild the auditions were, invited agents, producers, directors, and Broadway stars to judge and pick the finalists. I passed two auditions successfully and almost blew my chance for the finals by attempting the tart's speech in John Steinbeck's *The Moon Is Down*. Emphasizing my character's social disease, I smeared patches of liver-colored greasepaint on the corners of my mouth and under my eyes (imitating Claire Trevor in *Dead End*). Mr. Kaufman stopped me after the first few lines. Running down the aisle, his arms flying, he shouted, "Oh, Jesus, kid! What are you pulling? Aren't you the kid who did the thing of being an orphan and having red hair?" (I had done "Anne of Green Gables" for my first audition.) His voice shot high with impatience.

"Yes," I admitted, my heart pounding. "I thought I'd do something with more range."

He shot me a look of pained dismay. "You don't pass for a hooker, kid. Now wait a second," he ordered, and climbed up to the stage, took me by the shoulders and, facing the audience of waiting applicants, said, "This kid is an example of what not to do. I'm trying to show you how to impress people by showing off the best of your talents. Don't smear up your mugs or dress in the wrong clothes. You'll give the wrong impression, confuse people, and lose out.

"Now you go off," he ordered, shoving me toward the exit. "Wash that crap off your puss and come back flashing freckles and do your monologue. What was it again?"

I came back, undaunted, and did my "Anne of Green Gables," which made me a finalist and a winner in the contest.

I was inundated with letters after the successful Golden auditions and wooed by talent scouts from Paramount Pictures and Warner Brothers. The letterheads from impressive theatrical managements sent me into rapturous delight. I was already counting my money and feeling quite dizzy from a spinning sensation of glory. Choices had to be made. The one momentous decision that brought me down to earth with a crash involved giving up the Neighborhood Playhouse. But I had pushed myself this far and couldn't stay in school any longer. I was determined to see my ambitions through and become a professional actress. I set up a round of interviews.

Answering all the letters I received, I met the high and the mighty as well as the mountebanks. One talent scout in particular made an impression, perhaps because he posed for me the problem of which path to follow. His name was something like Kelley or Flynn, and he operated out of a tiny, ill-lit office cluttered with yellowing posters that a touch could reduce to a pile of dust. His desk was so cluttered with God only knows how many years of actors' résumés and glossy photographs that I could barely distinguish his face between the mounds of paper.

"I caught your act at the Golden," he said as he pressed out a cigarette after using it to light up another. "You're a talented kid. What are you, Irish?"

"I'm part Irish," I said.

"Oh yeah, well, that's the good part," he said. "You got an agent yet, kid?"

"Not yet," I answered, "But I'm auditioning for the road company of *The Cherry Orchard*." I had received a letter from Peggy Webster, the director, and my cronies from the Playhouse advised me to go after that job.

"What's that? That Russian play?" he asked. I didn't even answer and he continued, "Jeeze, what do you want to get involved with the Russkis for?" His eyes danced like Aunt Mary's. "You could have a great future in movies."

The question stopped me cold. Would I choose to be Irish and commercial or Slavic and arty? But by this time there was no question. I answered defensively, "I have to start supporting myself and if I can get a job touring in a play, I can save some money."

"Let me give you a piece of friendly advice, kid. Never put on a poor mouth. Keep your nose clean and you'll go far in this business." At that he hiked up his trousers and winked at me. I don't know why that bit of advice made such an impression on me, but it did.

When I signed the contract for the road tour of *The Cherry Orchard,* Katherine and Boris were delighted because I was doing Chekhov. But when I called my father and told him of my good fortune he said, "Well, daughts, if that's what you really want. You're out of nest now so of course I have to submit. I suppose your interest in the science was passing fancy for you or maybe you were seduced by money and glamour. All right. That's all. You have **my** blessing."

I hung up and burst into tears. I was ashamed to have bragged to him that the job paid seventy-five dollars a week, a sum exceeding his present salary. I knew I had disappointed him with my choice of profession, and I felt guilty about going so far from my mother.

When I returned from the tour some months later, I joined my sisters on a visit to my mother at the State Hospital in Wingdale. I carried the bag Katherine brought, which held a cream cheese sandwich and a ripe banana. Bananas were my mother's favorite food, and she was eating more of them now because she had had her teeth pulled and was having trouble being fitted for false ones. The last time I had visited, she was ashamed to smile or kiss us and kept covering her mouth with her hand.

The ground was frozen under the snow. Katherine was pregnant, so Beady and I each held an elbow and led her up the hill to the door of the hospital. Icy patches and ridges of frozen mud made walking hazardous. A fierce wind tangled our hair and lashed at our faces. We had to force our way against it and were all but blown through the hospital doors.

We stopped at the front desk to register when a nurse appeared. She looked from Katherine's belly to Beady and then to me. She seemed unsure; her voice went very low, almost to a whisper; "Are you the Jackson girls?" she asked. It seemed ages before she continued. "Will you come with me to the administrator's office?" She held the door open, announced us, and slipped away.

The man behind the desk was fingering through forms. His eyes went to Katherine first, taking in her condition, and then he quickly lowered his head and gazed down at his papers.

"Just take any seat." The procedure was unusual. Beady caught the mood and Katherine and I too grew anxious and suspicious. We sat ready for the blow — and it came.

"I'm sorry you girls had to take this trip on a day like today. Your mother, Mrs. Jackson, passed away this morning. I've already informed your father. He'll be coming up to take care of the details." He explained more about her condition, that whatever she had "became acute and she didn't respond to medication." But we already knew all we needed to know — she was gone.

My sisters' voices cracked in a duet of grief which

went from a high pitch of stunned disbelief to the awful deep notes which surge up from way inside and rack the body. I went to stone. I couldn't cry, because I was with a stranger and I became inhibited by his discomfort at such raw emotion. I sat with the sandwich bag on my lap. The heat in the room brought out the smell of the banana.

He offered to let us wait in his outer office till visiting hours were over and we could catch our bus back home.

Daddy looked terribly pale when I saw him that evening at Katherine's. The blood was drained from his face. Boris took his arm and they left to make funeral arrangements.

On that awful day, I arrived at the funeral parlor before my sisters. I went in to the receiving room to view the body and came right back out. The figure in the coffin was not my mother. "Where's Mrs. Jackson?" I asked the man in black mourning tails and he raised his arm in a ceremonial sweep toward the room I had just left. I hadn't recognized her. They'd curled her hair, rouged her cheeks, and painted her mouth. When I finally saw behind the mortician's mask and recognized Mom's own face, her features blurred before my tears. I touched my lips to her forehead and sobbed. Katherine appeared and held me to her. Beady was holding Daddy's hand. Aunt Gert, Uncle Otto, and Aunt Anne arrived to console us; Bea's and Katherine's in-laws came, as did our neighbor Mrs. Ellensburg. There was a decent showing of mourners on that grey and bitter cold day. But cold as it was, it was a relief to get into the bracing air after the heavy flowery smell of the funeral parlor, if only to join the procession of black cars to the crematorium.

The crematorium was a small room decorated with white lilies and orange gladioli on an altar, and there were folding chairs to sit in. We all felt awkward and uneasy about the details. What would be done with the remains? Would the urn be buried? We deferred to Dad throughout the whole ordeal.

When Aunt Maggie in Pittsburgh heard about the funeral arrangements, the telephone wires sizzled between New York and Pittsburgh. She was the dearest and calmest woman in the entire Murray clan, and she had Ma'am's gentleness and beautiful manners. But when she phoned Daddy about the cremation her voice could be heard throughout Katherine's house. "John," she said, "You're a fiend for not putting my sister in hallowed ground. You'll never live this down. As long as I'm on this earth, I'll never forgive you for this terrible wicked deed." The click from her slamming down the receiver shot through our ears, cutting us more than her words.

After Mom's death, Dad moved from Liberty Avenue to Astoria, where he lived in the back room of his shop and hired someone to cook and clean. There certainly was a change in him. Before, he had drawn a definite line between his business and home life, but now he expressed himself openly everywhere. He wore colorful ties and a flower on the lapel of his barber's smock. He displayed a collection of antiques as well as his musical instruments in the shop, and even practiced between customers. His black teakwood and mother-of-pearl chair sat in a corner of the shop and his hand-painted china was neatly arranged in the window. All in all, he presented himself to the world as a free spirit.

The widow who used to come to clean began staying for longer periods, and Dad had some of the "female companionship" he'd been missing for the past few years.

Twice widowed, Mrs. Mitchell was submissive and servile, and very ill at ease with Katherine, Beady, and me. She called our father "Johnny" and the intimacy offended and shocked us.

When Katherine gave birth to a son, the first male child in our family, Pop became an ecstatic grandfather. The event rekindled his family feelings and he began writing "Dear Son" letters to Emil, who was away in the service:

Dear Son Emil,

Pop Jackson is having honor to address you as Son. Yesterday me and Bea was at your people's house. I'm happy to tell you your father is well versed in knowing underdog's struggle. We (I feel) are real comrades. We had good time. Laugh and more laugh. Of course, ever so often mine thoughts switch to you two sons. Our comrades Soviets are doing fine job. They are almost as good as us.

Dear Emil, please don't forget even if it is one cent postcard write to your mother. I don't know if you do know what it means to her. I told Boris same thing too.

Beatrice thought proper to send you razors which you will receive under special cover, including a razor strop, which is my inspiration. You can strop your razor, at the same time you get it. Use only canvas (not the leather side) 8-10 strokes is enough. It will probably take time but keep on sharpening them. I am sending today or in very near future about 30 razors to USSR God Bless them. They are doing fine job knocking stuffing out of Nazies.

Dear Son, I don't want to be super anything, I do strive to be realist. There is so many things to be done, busy all the time. Business as usual. It is not meant for me to get rich in material sense. Spiritually I own biggest part of the world. This morning at 2 a.m. I had to get up my foot was aching me. I got myself cup of coffee and I started to meditate. That is why I am going to write 3 long letters. Accordion is doing good. I play faithfully about 2½ hours every day. We have plenty fun only it is hard to take around.

Your brother is making portrait of your wife. What a knockout. You will be as proud as a peacock when you see it. He is artist of high rating. I told him that I have one more daughter. Of course, I have nothing to do with any match-making, I had to say something.

I'll end with Cheerio, your Pop,

John Jackson

But Pop had no luck as a matchmaker for me. Beady was pregnant and moved in with Katherine until her husband, Emil, came home. I found a room of my own on Eleventh Street and Fifth Avenue. The *Cherry Orchard* tour which launched me in the theatre had changed my life, and I had forgotten the overtures from Hollywood and had dedicated myself to a life on the stage. My room, which was in an elegant Stanford White building, was to be the base for my conquest of Broadway. It, and three others like it, were formerly the maids' quarters for the opulent apartments above. The room was very small with enormously high ceilings. I often reflected that if I could only have turned the place on its side, I would have had plenty of space to ramble about in. The bathroom in the hall outside my door had a beautiful leaded window overlooking the courtyard and a tub over six feet long. The sense of privacy was exquisite.

For the first week or so in my new room, I left a night-light on and jumped at every noise. But once I met and talked to my only neighbors down the hall, two charming sisters, I began to feel more comfortable. They became buffers for my loneliness.

As familiarity set in, after a week or so, I braved padding about in my bare feet to my bathroom. One evening, I left my door ajar and, clad only in my slip or nightie, I laundered and listened to my radio. The blare of music and the sloshing of water drowned out all other sound, so that I didn't hear the click of heels in the hallway.

I looked up and was startled by the apparition in my bathroom doorway. One hand on her hip, the other leaning on the door jamb, a woman stood there in an orange dress, her hair the color of iodine. The dress's neckline plunged down to a wide, tightly pulled belt, held shut by a paper clip. I froze, bent over the sink. "What the hell do you think you're doing?" she boomed in a voice shot with whiskey and cigarettes. She was a Toulouse-Lautrec come to life.

I was rendered mute at first. When I finally screeched, she mumbled, "Oh shit," and then went into my room and slammed the door. I was locked out.

Like a bird escaping a cat, I flew to my neighbor's. "Yvette," I screamed and pounded wildly on her door. She had only a step to walk from any position in her tiny compartment, so she was quick to unlatch her door and draw me in. "Some woman is in my room," I gasped. "She's locked me out. I think she's drunk or crazy."

Yvette looked at me knowingly and then said, "It's probably Lila. She used to have your room but she was dispossessed. They locked her out months ago. This is the second time she's tried this. You're lucky the men have stopped coming. We had to get Felix, the elevator operator, to throw her out the last time." Felix was so close to senility that I couldn't imagine him being much help. "Just stay put, and we'll wait her out," Yvette advised.

Neither of us went for help because we were both in nightclothes and the pay phone was on the fourth floor. As it turned out, it wasn't necessary. The lady Lila soon left, shouting obscenities and laughing raucously. She knocked loudly on Yvette's door, seeming to enjoy the discomfort she had caused, before she made her exit.

Too keyed up to sleep, Yvette and I sat and talked into the night. She made me instant coffee, which she prepared on a hot plate resting on a board over her bathtub. A full kitchen was incorporated in that tiny dwelling. I couldn't wait to borrow ideas for a bathroom-kitchen from her.

The months flew by. I played in a series of flops, going from one job to another in such rapid succession I had no time to mourn over failures. When I left town for tryouts or went to summer stock for a summer, I'd sublet my room. At one point I rented it to Marlon Brando, and considered it an honor to have him as a tenant. Every actor in New York envied and admired him. It turned out to be a bit of a nuisance, though, because when he moved out on my return, I was annoyed by phone calls and visits from the most unlikely characters, mostly women.

Marlon did send me a blessing, though, in the person of Wally Cox, who came down my hall one evening looking for him and instead found me at my laundering. He was an adorable man and I liked him immediately. I asked him in and gave him Uneeda Biscuits, American cheese, and wine, and we stayed up talking and laughing until the wee hours. He invited confidence and we became close friends.

I dated older men for a while. My field was narrow; most of my peers were either still in the army or about to be drafted. And then in 1946 I met Elijah (Hebrew for "God"). He was just back from the medical corps overseas and was still wearing his captain's uniform. We were cast together in a showcase production of *This Property Is Condemned* by Tennessee Williams. My dressing room was a coal bin in the cellar of the Hudson Street Library; Eli's was a neighboring bin. He brought me daffodils one evening and we ate late supper at the Humpty Dumpty Diner on Seventh Avenue in Greenwich Village. In the back of my mind I knew right then I'd marry him. We had a lot in common: neither of us could sing; both of us loved to act; we were both ambitious and idealistic; and we endowed each other with the most extraordinary virtues.

We were in bed one cold Sunday morning when a knock came at the door of my ground-floor room.

"Who's there?" I asked groggily.

"Citizen John Jackson," came the retort. Eli and I sat bolt upright.

"Just a minute, Pop," I said, as Eli dressed frantically and jumped out the window into the alley. By the time I opened the door, Citizen John had left.

When I called Katherine later, she told me, "Oh yes, Pop called. He said he didn't think you were alone and he saw a man running down the street in the snow, combing his hair."

If Pop ever recognized Eli as the man fleeing in the snow, he never let on. They met about six months later in Dad's shop in Astoria. I prepared Eli for our visit, but I knew better than to try to influence my father beforehand. Although I felt confident and proud to present Eli, I was nevertheless nervous about introducing him. My father greeted us in his barber smock with a bachelor button on his lapel. He hung the closing sign on the shop door and ushered us in brusquely. Daddy had an irritating way of sizing people up, which caused me acute embarrassment. He was abrupt, and the bevy of rapid-fire questions followed by sidewise glances could be even more unnerving.

"Speak up. Where is father from? How long is he in America? Where in Poland? How is your Yiddish? Do you speak little German?"

It was a technique designed to throw the other person off guard. But Eli met the occasion. He openly enjoyed my father and disarmed him in turn by his charm and good manners.

His parents were born in Galicia, Poland, he said. His father came to America in the twenties, was a tailor by trade and then ran a candy store in the Red Hook section of Brooklyn. All four children were college graduates — three were Phi Beta Kappa.

Daddy was impressed; a working-class family's children with an education. What could be better?

He offered to "cut the hairs and would you like shave and facial?" Eli declined the facial but accepted the haircut. Daddy then cranked the barber chair, unfurled the hair cloth, and with one flourish covered his client. They discussed the war, Roosevelt's death, Hitler's defeat, and the victory of the Allies. Daddy was impressed with Eli's service record. "A captain in the medics. Oi yoy yoy," Pop said, shaking his head in admiration. All kinds of tonics were presented for Eli to sniff and select. He was given the royal treatment. My father whistled and sang as he frisked about and then he vigorously massaged Eli's head. After sweeping up the black curls, Pop brought out the wine and his accordion, and sang to his own accompaniment. We stayed long into the night. Clearly, Eli passed the test with flying colors.

At our wedding party in March, 1948, my father donned his new grey pin-striped suit and brought gifts of lipstick to all the women. I inherited a wonderful new family, and although we are a "mixed" marriage, we were spared the unpleasantness that sometimes results from religious differences. When we were still struggling actors, I became pregnant. I had been Jean Arthur's understudy in the play *Peter Pan*. Peter, our son, was born February 20, 1951. This period was fraught with joy and pain. It was for me a beginning of motherhood and also the beginning of my father's illness.

My father had gone into Queens General Hospital for a checkup, which sounded harmless enough at the time. When we visited him there, it didn't seem unnatural to see him in the white hospital gown because it resembled his barber's uniform. His bare legs, blond, hairy, and too white and muscular, did look queer as he shuffled about in paper mules. My sisters sat on the foot of his bed and I leaned on the radiator. We all tried to be cheery, casual, and not give the impression that we were apprehensive, that we all harbored horrible hospital memories. Katherine patted Pop on the cheeks and cooed affectionately, "Boris sends his love, hon. He had to work tonight but he'll be coming to see you."

"No need. No obligation. I'll be leaving in day or two." Daddy was abrupt.

"Emil's working too, you know, Pop, or he would have come. But as you say, you'll be back in the shop so he'll be in to see you for his haircut." Beady and Kay competed a lot for Pop's attention.

I felt the need to send Eli's regards, but my father hadn't yet developed the father-son relationship he had with Boris and Emil.

"Daddy," I asked, "how do you feel?"

"Not too hot. I don't like institutions of any kind. I don't trust sons of bitches . . . they only interested in grabbing the money. Whole system is cockeyed. So why should they be any different? Have you got cigarette, daughts?"

I gave my father a Pall Mall. My sister Katherine took one too and struck a match.

"Here's a light, hon," Katherine said, holding the match up for Pop. He shot her an impatient look for acting so solicitous.

"Do they allow smoking here?" Beady asked. "There are other patients in the ward, you know." There was an edge in her voice and she coughed and wrinkled her nose in annoyance, fanning off the smoke.

"Oh, they allow anything that keeps them in business. If cigarette makes you sick, you're in right place. Don't ask foolish questions, daughts."

Beady pursed her mouth and shot Pop her squinty-eyed look.

"Would you like anything from downstairs?" I asked when we had finished our smoke. "A Dixie or some magazines or a newspaper?"

"Don't be fidgety," he said. "No I don't want Dixie. I don't like sweets; you know that. Magazines I get from other patients. They're all junk anyway, and newspaper is all lies. I'm not interested in the murder of boys in Korea. Those people don't need us there. They prefer Yanks go home. Boy we got one hell of a nerve butting into their business."

There was silence for a while. Neither Katherine nor Beatrice wanted to be the next victim of Daddy's irritability. We all exchanged sympathetic and knowing looks and waited for the conversation to turn to a safe subject.

Once Pop had cowed both Beatrice and me he was

perfectly dear. But he was above all fair, and Katherine was the only one of us who hadn't had her comeuppance. It was, of course, inevitable. If she was going to try to outwit him by her silence and diplomacy, he would set a trap. We all knew it had to happen.

"How's the Boris, Katrin?"

"He's fine, Pop, just fine, uh huh."

"Still confused about being capitalist?"

"Why, I don't know what you mean," my sister said and her nostrils flared.

"Why he couldn't teach the Russian literature? Why he had to go into business with the father? Well, of course, that's your affair and his. But still . . ."

"Look, Daddy, I don't want to get into this discussion, O.K.? You know how Mr. Egorenkov is and you know how Boris is. So don't start, O.K.?"

"Of course, I know." In the silence that fell we all looked at the clock. The visiting hours seemed interminable. We waited anxiously for the nurses to start hurrying us out, though Dad seemed intent on keeping us there.

"I don't like to ask favors, you know that. But I could use clean shirt to go home in."

"Of course, Pop," Beady and I chimed in unison. Katherine didn't reply, still vexed by the near blow-up.

"No," Pop said in a rather conniving voice. "I prefer the Katrin to call Mrs. Mitchell. She'll wash the shirt for me." Mrs. Mitchell's name hung heavy in the air. Katherine promised to call her, although it meant waiting for her to come to the candy store phone. My sister resented, as we all did, having to deal with her. We couldn't understand what Daddy saw in her. She seemed to us ill equipped to capture one man, let alone two, and being twice a merry widow, she was now setting her cap for a third.

When the visiting time was finally up, we all three kissed Pop's cheek. He was pleased at the attention, but feigned annoyance. "All right. Let's not have foolish sentimentality. You know I don't go in for the mush."

The bell rang and we started hustling toward the door.

"Call us when you get back to your shop, Pop," Beady said.

"Yeah, give the regards to my sons and, Katrin, don't forget the call to the Mitchell."

As we waited for the elevator, I saw the intern on his way to make some rounds. Excusing myself from Katherine and Beady, who went on home, I approached the doctor and introduced myself, then asked, "Can you tell me who's been seeing my father and what the trouble is?"

"Jackson," he said frowning and looking at his chart. "Oh, right, John Jackson." He shuffled through his papers of reports and charts as I watched carefully, trying to read his expression.

"He's in for observation," the young man said, glancing toward the ward, obviously thinking I should be satisfied with that explanation. The smell of the hospital and the slow, still breath of the sick permeated the air. The corridor filled with hospital noises, rattling steel trays and beds being rolled around, nurses whispering and bustling about.

"What are you looking for?" I asked. The steadiness of my voice surprised me.

The young intern kept his head turned away from me; he apparently resented my questioning. There was a moment of hesitation as he debated with himself whether to consult the chart or to just tell me. And then he said it: "Cancer."

"Oh. Thank you, doctor," I managed evenly, and we walked off in different directions.

In the elevator I just shut my eyes trying to breathe evenly and calmly. I didn't want to tell my sisters before we sought another opinion.

So Daddy went from Queens Hospital to a Park Avenue doctor, and the diagnosis remained the same. He was operated on, and we were told that he'd have about two years to live. My sisters and I decided not to tell Pop what we knew.

He stayed at the apartment behind his shop and tried working for a while, but the pain soon worsened; he needed stronger and stronger drugs, and finally he lived with first one daughter and then the other. He tried to be cheery and pleasant with us and the frolicking grandchildren, but he tactfully let us know that he knew the nature of his illness. We seldom saw his spirits flag, however. He came to see me in Shaw's *Arms and the Man,* and afterward he set up a home movie starring himself with his three daughters. He'd put on his good grey pin-striped suit for the evening and we could see how he had shrunk inside it so that the pants bagged and the jacket fell off his shoulders, fitting loosely over his chest and stomach. As he continued to lose weight, his ears protruded, his horn-rimmed glasses fell forward on his nose, and the skin on his head pulled tighter. His cheekbones became more prominent and he neglected to fix a side tooth that had lost its inlay. There were no more nights at the Yugoslav club, no more wine, and only rarely did he play his accordion. With Mom gone and his girls grown and married, he waited for the end.

Dad returned to the hospital for the last weeks of his life. He joked with the doctors about losing his testicles and growing breasts from the hormone treatments, but I sensed an embarrassment when he talked about it. He maintained a strong bravado for us; he told us about the bet he had with the man in the bed across the aisle on which of them would go first. His antagonism to the doctors softened; he was in their hands and as a "man of science," he analyzed his illness and described the effects of the different drugs. When he was feeling well enough, he tried to relieve my tension by talking about his life and destiny.

"I'm writing memoirs, Anna," he said, during what was to be the last visit before all the tubes went into him and life drained out. "And I want to say only this. I have not regretted any part of my life. If I had to do whole thing over, I would not change or regret it. I'm leaving each of you girls one dollar — that's not out of vengeance, that's out of necessity. You remember I always told you, children have to learn to swim or drown. Birds must leave nests. We did the best we knew how, the mother and me. Circumstances didn't allow us to do more or better. Go over there, in brown bag in drawer is harmonica. Give to the Peter; he's little fellow, I know, but he's never too young for make the music."

I went to the dresser in Pop's corner and took the harmonica from the brown bag. I saw a white pad and recognized my father's handwriting. The title read, "Joy of Finding." It was his memoirs.

"Daddy, is there something you want before I leave?"

"No, daughts," he said. "Well, pain is quite bad at night," he continued quietly, with great effort; "I think I'd like night nurse."

I called my sisters when I left that day and alerted them. Aunt Gert flew in from Pittsburgh. We called Uncle Otto to warn him. For the next week Daddy was inaccessible to us, though we were allowed to see him, with the tubes and bottles hanging menacingly over him. The nurses walked in and out and spoke in hushed tones, giving us wan and sympathetic smiles as they passed. Aunt Gert came to the hospital with me one night, and at the elevator she said, "Anna, I think you better expect . . . well, he won't last long."

I was in class at the Actors' Studio the next day when Eli opened the side door and caught my eye. He looked worried and motioned me to follow him to an empty rehearsal room down the hall. "The hospital called. Your father died," he told me gently, holding me to him. For one weak moment my knees buckled and my throat constricted. Eli guided me out past the actors mingling in the outer hall to the subway and home.

I read "Joy of Finding" after the funeral. "It's writer's profound wish to depict without any flowering, truth as it happened," it began. Right on cue, as I finished the unfinished manuscript, my son Peter began blowing on my father's harmonica. And I had to smile, because even though Peter was only one and a half years old, it sounded just like Pop practicing.